STAR TREK
THE ENTERPRISE LOGS

WARNING: THIS MATERIAL IS CLASSIFIED. FAILURE TO COMPLY
WITH SECURITY AND CLASSIFICATION PROCEDURES IS ILLEGAL
AND PUNISHABLE ACCORDING TO *SECURITY ACT KR/UFP 3.1*

GOLDEN PRESS
Western Publishing Company, Inc.   Racine, Wisconsin.

PSYCHO-FILE

42 GRAPHICS and
27 MAGNE-TAPES,
DO NOT DE-MAG!

SUBJECT: KIRK,
JAMES T.,
CAPTAIN, SSC
SF SERVICE NUMBER:
947-0176, CEC

NOT FOR COPYING!
(EXCEPT WHEN AUTHORIZED BY
SF SECURITY AND SUBJECT'S
IMMEDIATE SUPERIOR OFFICER.)

IDENTI-FAX

KIRK, JAMES T.

SC-937-0176, CEC

| L-1 | L-2 | L-3 | L-4 | L-5 |

R-1 R-2 R-3 R-4 R-5

HGT—5'11
WGT—173

IDENTIFYING MARKS

FLASHBURN, LEFT UPPER ARM, PHASER-3 SCAR RIGHT KNEE, TWO REPAIRED
FRACTURES, LOWER RIGHT LEG; SURGICAL-LASER SCAR, SPINAL BASE;
ONE MAGNESIUM SPINAL DISC

SON OF GREAT KLINGON WAR HERO ACCEPTS MEDAL

JAMES T. KIRK, 12, ONLY
SURVIVING SON OF COL.
BENJAMIN KIRK, HERO OF
THE **KLINGON REPULSION**,
RECEIVING FATHER'S
POSTHUMOUS SUPREME
MEDAL OF HONOR, ONLY
THE 4TH AWARDED IN
TWO CENTURIES. YOUNG
KIRK HAS ALSO BEEN
ASSURED APPOINTMENT
TO THE SPACE ACADEMY
ON COMPLETION OF PREP
STUDIES.

UNITED FEDERATION
OF PLANETS
SPACE ACADEMY

APPOINTMENT
TO ACADEMY

KNOW ALL BY THIS CERTIFICATE THAT
JAMES T. KIRK

HAS BEEN ACCEPTED FOR FULL
MATRICULATION AT THIS INSTITUTE
AND, FOR THE DURATION, SHALL BE
ENTITLED TO THE RANK AND
COMPENSATION OF A TRAINEE-STAR
FLEET OFFICER. IN RECOGNITION OF
THIS APPOINTMENT I AFFIX MY
SEAL AND HAND.

Alden McWilliams

COMMANDER
UFP SPACE ACADEMY

"Subject entered as youngest
member of his class and
suffered **ADDITIONAL** pressure due to
the nature of his appointment!"

THAT'S WHAT I SAID,
KIRK—YOU'RE HERE
ON A **PASS**! A SON-OF-
SERVICE-HERO PASS!

YOU'RE
ENTITLED TO
YOUR OPINION,
ROGGE!

MIGHT AS WELL TAKE HIM
ON, JIM, OR HE'LL BE AT IT
FOR THE NEXT FOUR YEARS!

IT WILL
BLOW OVER,
HUX!

LOOK OUT,
KIRK!

"The warning from
another cadet came
not a second too soon!"

"They proceeded by Nuke-mobile to the Enterprise's Transporter-Rendezvous-Point..."

NOT A WORD FROM EITHER OF THEM! THAT'S NORMAL FOR THE VULCAN! BUT THIS FELLOW SCOTT...

BLAST! TROUBLE-LIGHT! COOLANT COILS OVER-HEATING!

I DIDN'T BRING A THERMI-SENSOR! IT'LL TAKE ME HOURS TO FIND THE LEAK WITHOUT ONE!

THERE'S A GOOD CHANCE IT'S IN THE THIRD DIVERTER, MR. SCOTT!

LOOK, SON--UHH, I MEAN, CAPTAIN-- I'VE GOT TWO DEGREES IN ENGINEERING I EARNED THE HARD WAY! AND I STRIPPED MY FIRST NUKE-V-3 WHEN I WAS 12!

YES OF COURSE, LIEUTENANT! BUT THIS IS A V-3/A, BUILT WITHIN THE PAST TWO YEARS! THEY ISSUED A WARNING--

--LAST WEEK AGAINST A DEFECT IN THE 3RD DIVER-TER SYSTEM OF ALL V-3/As!

AHHH, I WAS LOCKED IN WITH A SICK INTAKE VALVE ALL LAST WEEK! I MISSED IT!

"With the repair swiftly completed."

WHAT KIND OF SPIRIT IS YOUR PLEASURE, CAPTAIN?

I'M NOT MUCH OF A DRINKING MAN, SCOTTY!

I THINK MR. SCOTT MAY FIND IT IN HIS HEART TO FORGIVE YOU THAT, SIR!

"Lt. Scott fashioned a handsome 'medal' for Captain Kirk--"

TO CAPT. J KIRK FOR KNOWING HIS WAY OUT OF A NUKE V-3 ENGINE ORDER OF THE BATTERED OIL CAN

"from the flattened and buffed section of a V-3/A Diverter!"

STAR TREK— THE PLANET OF NO RETURN

THE SUCTION FIELD... IT'S BEING CREATED BY A--A GIANT *CANNIBAL PLANT!*

TRY...TRY TO BREAK *FREE*...OR THAT AWE-SOME THING WILL DEVOUR US ALL!

IT WAS THE STRANGEST CIVILIZATION IN ALL THE KNOWN UNIVERSE -- MORE AWESOME THAN THE MIND OF MAN COULD CONCEIVE! AND THE EXPEDITION TEAM FROM THE STAR SPACESHIP *USS ENTERPRISE* SOON REGRETTED THEIR DECISION TO EXPLORE K-G...

Captain's Log, Stardate 18:09.2 .... DATA REF.... 1.00-1.26

CAPTAIN'S LOG, STAR DATE 18:09.2— ENTERPRISE CARRYING OUT EXPLORATION MISSION THROUGH GALAXY ALPHA. SO FAR WE'VE SEEN NO INDICATION OF LIFE ANYWHERE IN THE GALAXY...

CAPT. KIRK, SIR-- I'VE PICKED UP AN-OTHER CELESTIAL BODY ON THE SPACE-SCOPE! AND THIS ONE APPEARS *FERTILE!*

GIVE ME A CLOSEUP OF IT ON THE TV *SCANNER!*

LOOK AT HER, CAPTAIN... *KELLY GREEN* ...STEEPED IN VEGETATION!

YES...MUCH MORE SO THAN OUR OWN EARTH! IF THERE'S LIFE IN THIS GALAXY, WE'LL FIND IT THERE...

ATTENTION CREW! WE'RE GOING TO DISPATCH AN EXPLORATION PARTY! MAKE NECESSARY PREPARATIONS!

AS THE *ENTERPRISE* CLOSES ON THE PLANET, SHE PASSES THROUGH AN EERIE SPACE FOG...

...A MIST WITHIN WHICH FLOAT A HANDFUL OF STRANGE PLANT SPORES THAT FASTEN ONTO THE HULL OF THE SHIP...

THE ONE-CELLED REPRODUCTIVE BODIES ARE SO MINUTE, YET SO POWERFUL, THAT THEY SEEP THROUGH THE VERY SUPERSTRUCTURE...

LET'S SEE WHAT THE CAPTAIN ORDERED FOR THE EXPLORATION TEAM, A THREE-DAY SUPPLY OF FOOD CONCENTRATE... WATER CAPSULES...

SUDDENLY...

VERY STRANGE! LET US OBSERVE THEM, DR. McCOY...

LISTEN TO *THAT!* WHAT IN THE *WILD HEAVENS* HAS GOTTEN INTO THOSE GUINEA PIGS..?

SQUEEEK!

SQUEEK SQUEEK!

THE TWO MEN TURN - THEIR EYES FALL ON A STARTLING SIGHT...

THEY'RE MAKING A FANTASTIC TRANS-FORMATION OF SOME KIND! IT'S AS IF—

AS IF THEY'RE TURNING INTO *PLANTS!* WE'VE *GOT TO* RECORD THIS ON FILM FOR FUTURE RESEARCH REFERENCE...

BUT BEFORE DR. McCOY CAN ACT, A MENACE NO MORTAL MAN HAS EVER KNOWN EXPLODES FROM THE CAGE AND...

AND THEY ARE ON A RAMPAGE-- OUT TO DESTROY US BOTH! *GUARDS! GUARDS!*

T-THE ANIMALS...THEY'VE TRANS-FORMED INTO *GIANT, HOSTILE TREES!*

THE CAPTAIN AND DR. McCOY JOIN THE EXPLORATION TEAM IN THE *TELEPORTATION CHAMBER!* BEAMS FROM ABOVE SUDDENLY ILLUMINATE THEIR BODIES AND THEN...

HERE WE GO--- WE'LL MAKE AN HOURLY TV-RADIO REPORT TO THE HOVERING SHIP, MR. SPOCK!

WE WILL ANXIOUSLY BE AWAITING YOUR WORD, CAPTAIN! MAY LUCK BE WITH YOU...

AN INSTANT LATER, THE FIVE ARE TELEPORTED THROUGH SPACE TO RE-APPEAR ON THE CELESTIAL BODY THEY NOW REFER TO OFFICIALLY AS *PLANET K-G**...

JUST LOOK AT THE COLOFUL VEGETATION-- ISN'T IT MAGNIFICENT!

YES, JANICE--ALMOST UNBELIEVABLE! WELL, LET'S FAN OUT AND RECONNOITER THE AREA FOR POSSIBLE *INTELLIGENT LIFE* HERE...

*PLANET K-G -- PLANET KELLY GREEN.

THE TEAM MOVES ACROSS THE *CLEARING!* AS THEY DO SO, CREWMAN HUNT PASSES THROUGH A PATCH OF MIST...

AND AS THE GROUP REACHES THE THICK, MULTICOLORED FOLIAGE...

ALL RIGHT--NOW WE'LL REGROUP AND... *HUNT! WHAT IN HEAVEN HAS HAPPENED TO YOU?*

I-I DON'T KNOW ...FEEL STRANGE...

EEEEK! HE'S CHANGING...INTO A-A PLANT!

JUST LIKE THE GUINEA PIGS BACK ON THE SHIP! HUNT! CAN YOU UNDERSTAND ME?

BUT THERE IS NO TIME FOR A REPLY-- FOR AT THAT MOMENT...

HEY! SOMETHING'S DRAWING US BACK... BUT WHAT?

DON'T KNOW, DEAN...BUT THE FORCE IS TOO STRONG TO RESIST...

THEN, TERROR SHAKES THE FOURSOME AS...

HOWLING COMETS! THIS SUCTION FORCE IS BEING CREATED BY A GIANT CANNIBAL PLANT! AND IT DREW THE WEAPONS RIGHT OUT OF OUR HANDS!

TRY...TRY TO BREAK FREE...OR THE THING WILL DEVOUR US IN SECONDS!

IT'S NO USE...THE MONSTER'S GOT US ALL...

WHAT A WAY TO DIE!

SUDDENLY...

THERE'S YOUR ANSWER! LOOK!

THE SUCTION FORCE...IT'S SUDDENLY STOPPED! BUT WHY?

THE PLANT TREE... IT'S WAVERING...

THE BATTLE MUST HAVE BEEN TOO MUCH FOR IT... IT *EXHAUSTED* ITSELF...

TIM-BER!

ALL RIGHT, TEAM-- LET'S GET BACK THERE AND START SEARCHING THE AREA FOR HUNT! HE'S GOT TO BE NEARBY...

CRAAASH

I'LL CHECK OUT THAT SIDE OF THE CLEARING...

WAIT! THAT... WON'T BE NECESSARY, DEAN! I'VE... I'VE FOUND HUNT!

WHY...ISN'T THAT...

YES, HUNT'S IDENTIFICATION BRACELET! THE PLANT TREE WAS HIM-- FULLY TRANSFORMED!

O-OH! HOW TERRIBLE...

EVEN THOUGH POOR HUNT WAS NO LONGER HUMAN, HE RETAINED ENOUGH INTELLIGENCE TO REALIZE OUR LIVES WERE IN DANGER...

THAT'S WHY HE ATTACKED THE CANNIBAL PLANT--TO SAVE US! AND HE DIED DOING IT!

A- A COMMUNITY OF VEGETATION... HOUSES... BUILDINGS... JUST AS WE HAVE ON EARTH!

FANTASTIC! THIS PLANT LIFE AN *INTELLIGENT SOCIETY* -- LISTEN! THEY'RE ACTUALLY COMMUNICATING WITH ONE ANOTHER! LET'S GO DOWN FOR A CLOSER LOOK...

WHEEEEE...

FLUTTER

FLUTTER

SUDDENLY...

THE TREES...THEY'RE MOVING...CLOSING IN ON US!

PROBABLY SENTRIES! START TRIGGERING... WE'VE GOT TO BLAST OUR WAY OUT OF THIS FIX!

CONCENTRATE OUR FIRE ON ONE SPECIFIC AREA... OPEN A HOLE IN THEIR RANKS BIG ENOUGH TO SLIP OUT OF HERE...

ZAAAP!

ZAAAP!

THE CONCENTRATED BARRAGE OF RAY FIRE SOON PAYS OFF AND...

WE'VE GOT OUR HOLE -- NOW TO GET THROUGH IT! ZERO IN ON THOSE GRASPING TREE LIMBS -- IF ONE OF THEM SNARES YOU YOU'RE *FINISHED!*

ZAAAP!

BREAKING OUT OF THE TREE TRAP, AN-OTHER DANGER IS SOON REALIZED...

HEY--HAVE A LOOK-SEE BEHIND US! SOME CRAZY WEEDS ARE AFTER US!

HMM-M...IT'S MY HUNCH THEY'RE TRAILING US LIKE BLOOD-HOUNDS... PROBABLY RE-LAYING OUR LOCATION BACK TO THEIR HEAD-QUARTERS...

WHRRRAP!

WRRRR!

WE'LL NEVER GET OUT OF HERE WITH THEM ON OUR TAILS—BLAST THEM TO PIECES!

YOU HIT EVERYONE IN SIGHT, CAPTAIN-- GOOD SHOOTING!

ZAAAP! ZAAAP!..... ZAAAP

I - I'M EXHAUSTED...

STEADY, HONEY-- I KNOW IT'S BEEN ROUGH...

THINK I SEE A CAV-ERN UP AHEAD! PER-HAPS WE CAN CATCH A BREATH OR TWO IN THERE...

TENSE MINUTES LATER, WITHIN A SMALL MOUNTAIN CAVERN...

LET'S FACE IT, CAPTAIN-- WE'RE TOO LITTLE IN NUMBER AND FIRE POWER TO FIGHT THIS... THIS INCREDIBLE NATION OF VEGETATION! WE MUST RETURN TO THE ENTERPRISE!

I READ YOU, DOC-TOR-- AND YOU'RE RIGHT!

AFTER WE CATCH OUR BREATH WE'LL GO OUTSIDE AND I'LL CON-TACT MR. SPOCK AND HAVE HIM MATERIALIZE US BACK TO THE SHIP!

AND I THOUGHT THIS PLANET WAS SO BEAUTIFUL-- IT'S THE UGLIEST PLACE I'VE EVER BEEN...

STAR TREK
THE PLANET OF NO RETURN PART II

THE EXPLORERS OF PLANET K-G GAPE IN AWE AS JANICE IS LOWERED INTO A BIZARRE CATTLE PEN BY THE RUNNING VINE PLANT!

HOLD IT...GIANT THORNS...THEY MAY BE POISONOUS!

S-SUFFERING STAR DUST--TH-THEY'RE PUTTING HER INTO SOME KIND OF AN *ANIMAL* ENCLOSURE!

HURRY! BLAST A PATH THROUGH THIS THORN ENTANGLEMENT! JANICE IS TRAPPED AMID A HORDE OF PLANETARY *BEASTS!*

THAT'S A BIG ENOUGH HOLE... *LET'S MOVE!*

ZAP!

BUT THEN...

G-GREAT GALLOPING GALAXIES! *N-NEW* THORNS... THE STEMS ARE SHOOTING OUT *FRESH* THORNS!

AGAIN, THE TRIO TRIGGERS THEIR WEAPONS...AND...

I-IT'S NO USE! SOME INCREDIBLE PLANT CHEMISTRY IS *REGENERATING* NEW GROWTHS AS FAST AS THE FORMER ONES DIE!

A...PROTECTIVE DEVICE...TO GUARD THE ANIMAL ENCLOSURE...

MAYBE THERE'S A BREAK IN THE THORN FENCE... AN ENTRANCE OF SOME KIND THAT WE CAN GET THROUGH!

SUDDENLY...

H-HOLD UP!

THE BEAST CREATURES...ON GRAZING GROUNDS...LIKE CATTLE!

AND THOSE ROLLING TUMBLEWEED-TYPE PLANTS...WH-WHY, THEY'RE ACTING AS *SHEEP DOGS!*

23

YES, ALIVE...BUT IF THEIR CATTLE BEASTS FEED ON THE LOWLY VEGETABLES... THAT MUST MEAN THE *SUPERIOR* PLANTS FEED ON THE *ANIMALS!* A-AND JANICE IS....

WITH THEM! THAT ROCK PINNACLE...IT WILL GIVE US A VIEW INTO THE CATTLE PEN!

I'VE GOT A GOOD SHOT INSIDE THE ENCLOSURE FROM HERE... LET'S SEE IF I CAN SPOT JANICE!

KIRK'S POWERFUL STELLAR BINOCU-LARS PIERCE THE CATTLE PEN...

I SEE HER...SHE'S HUDDLED AGAINST THE THORN BARRIER...BESIDE SOME SORT OF CHUTE AFFAIR...BUT, SO FAR, SHE'S *SAFE!*

THEN...

GR-GREAT GOSH! THAT THING'S A *CATTLE RUN*...I-I THINK THE BEASTS ARE BEING LED OUT...FOR *SLAUGHTER!*

A GROUP OF THEM ARE BEING LED OUT NOW! I-I'LL SEE WHAT *HAPPENS* TO THEM!

AND AS CAPTAIN KIRK OBSERVES FROM AFAR THROUGH THE BINOCULARS...

WOOO...

ZVIII...ZIIIIII

SLOWLY, THE GIANT TREES LOWER THEIR MASSIVE FOLIAGE CLUMPS...

THEN...

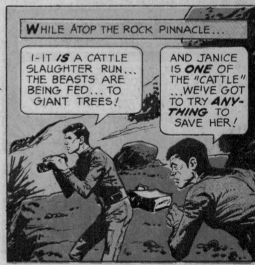

WHILE ATOP THE ROCK PINNACLE...

I-IT *IS* A CATTLE SLAUGHTER RUN... THE BEASTS ARE BEING FED... TO GIANT TREES!

AND JANICE IS *ONE* OF THE "CATTLE" ...WE'VE GOT TO TRY *ANYTHING* TO SAVE HER!

NO, WAIT! IT WON'T WORK, DOCTOR! WE'LL JUST DESTROY OURSELVES ON THOSE THORN GUARDS AND SACRIFICE JANICE ALSO!

ONLY MR. SPOCK ON THE ENTERPRISE CAN HELP JANICE NOW!

A FEW SECONDS LATER ON THE ENTERPRISE...

YOU WANT A LASER BEAM DESTRUCT RAY PIN-POINTED FOR AREA OF TEN YARDS, BUT THAT'S ALMOST IMPOSSIBLE, CAPTAIN KIRK!

IT'S GOT TO BE POSSIBLE, MR. SPOCK!

IF THE BEAM MISSES BY EVEN A FOOT IT CAN INCINERATE JANICE, AS WELL AS THE THORN GUARD FENCE! OUR BLAST GUNS AREN'T STRONG ENOUGH FOR THE JOB!

I SEE...

THEN IT IS A LIFE-AND-DEATH SHOT THAT MUST BE TAKEN! ALL RIGHT... SEND ME EXACT READINGS! IF YOU ARE A FRACTION OF AN INCH OFF WE WILL FAIL!

U.S.S. ENTERPRISE NCC-1701

CELESTIAL LONGITUDE 2,118... LATITUDE, 145.9...

THORN GUARD FENCE PRECISELY TEN FEET...SIX AND ONE HALF INCHES DEEP...

FENCE TEN FEET...SIX...ONE-HALF INCHES! WE WILL BE AT THE POINT OF BLAST IN THREE MINUTES!

DESPERATELY, THE TRIO RACES TOWARD THE LASER BEAM TARGET...

BUT *DON'T* WAIT FOR US, MR. SPOCK...THEY MAY BE TAKING JANICE *NOW!*

I WILL NOT WAIT, CAPTAIN KIRK...

...BUT I WILL NEED PRECIOUS SECONDS TO COMPUTE THE ENTERPRISE'S *PRE-CISE* POSITION RELATIVE TO TARGET!

WHIRRR... CLICK! CLICK!

AND MEANWHILE, WITHIN THE CATTLE ENCLOSURE...

TH-THEY THINK I'M ONE OF THEIR CATTLE BEASTS...GOT TO HOLD THEM OFF...THE MEN ARE TRYING TO HELP ME... TH-THEY *MUST BE!*

ZIIIII ZIIII

27

PRECIOUS MINUTES LATER, AS THE TRIO REACHES "GROUND ZERO"...

(PUFF PUFF) TH-THERE IT IS...THE CHUTE EXIT! — SPOCK'S BLAST SHOULD BURN A HOLE FIVE YARDS LONG IN IT...

IF ALL GOES WELL...

...BUT IF THE "SHEEPDOG" VINES LEAD JANICE *OUT* BEFORE HE TRIGGERS IT...WE'RE *SUNK!* — TO STOP *THEM* HE'LL HAVE TO HIT *JANICE* ALSO!

THEN...

TABULATIONS COMPLETE! BLAST BEAM IN FIVE SECONDS...FIVE...FOUR...

...THREE...TWO...

BLAST!

PRAY, GUYS ...*PRAY!*

As the doom spores fall, the exploring team begins to fade...

Then...

OROOO OROOO

And aboard the star space-ship Enterprise...

TH-THANK A THOUSAND STAR 'HEAVENS! THEY *MADE* IT!

OH, MR. SPOCK... LET'S GET *AWAY* FROM THIS DREADFUL PLANET *AT ONCE*, PLEASE!

YES! I SECOND THAT MOTION! (WHEW-W!)

NO!

IT CAN NOT BE DONE—*YET!* I HAVE CHARTED WHAT CAN HAPPEN IF THOSE GIANT TREES CONTINUE TO EMIT SPORES THROUGH THE UNIVERSE!

"THEY MAY FLOAT THROUGH SPACE FOR CENTURIES... EVEN LIGHT YEARS... BUT SOME DAY, SOMEWHERE THEY CAN STRIKE *OTHER* PLANETS..."

WHEN THEY *DO*, THAT VICTIM PLANET WILL *ALSO* BECOME A *K-G*... WITH KILLER, CANNIBAL PLANTS DEVOURING FOR FOOD *ALL LIFE UPON IT!*

BUT... *WHAT* IS THE SOLUTION?

WE MUST ORBIT THAT HIDEOUS LITTLE GLOBE UNTIL ALL FOLIAGE UPON IT IS DECIMATED BY OUR LASER BEAMS! I HAVE SET COURSE FOR THE MISSION ALREADY!

CAPTAIN'S LOG, STAR DATE 18:10.1 — WE ARE ORBITING THE PLANET KELLY GREEN, PERFORMING WHAT WILL BE OUR LAST DUTY HERE...

TOTAL DESTRUCTION— A MISSION THAT MUST BE FULFILLED BEFORE WE CAN CONTINUE OUR TOUR OF RESEARCH THROUGH THE VAST REACHES OF THE UNIVERSE...

CAPTAIN'S LOG, STAR DATE 19:03.4 -- ON THE OUTER FRINGE OF GALAXY NABU, CAME UPON A STRANGE BELT OF UNCHARTED ASTEROIDS--STRANGE FOR OBVIOUS REASONS...

GLOWING ASTEROIDS DOTTING THE ASTEROID BELT! NEVER SAW ANYTHING LIKE IT BEFORE, CAPTAIN!

YES, WELL WORTH LOOKING INTO, WOULDN'T YOU SAY, MR. SPOCK?

ANY UNEXPLAINABLE PHENOMENOM DEMANDS INVESTIGATION, CAPTAIN KIRK!

NAVIGATOR--SET A COURSE FOR THE CLOSEST OF THOSE GLOWING PLANETS!

THE ENTERPRISE KNIFES INTO THE ASTEROID BELT AND ZEROES IN ON ITS DESIRED TARGET...

WE'LL ORBIT THE PLANET AT ALTITUDE FIVE THOUSAND FEET FOR TELESCOPIC VIEWING AND PHOTOGRAPHING BEFORE DISPATCHING A LANDING PARTY!

SUDDENLY, THE MAMMOTH SPACESHIP IS ROCKED BY A POWERFUL TURBULENCE...

WHAT DID WE HIT?

NOTHING, CAPTAIN! BUT THE NEEDLES OF OUR CONTROL PANEL ARE FLUCTUATING WILDLY, INDICATING AN ATMOSPHERIC DISTURBANCE!

UP THE INFRA-RED PERISCOPE, CREWMAN -- AND LET'S SEE WHAT KIND OF DISTURBANCE IS OUT THERE!

YES, SIR!

HOWLING COMETS! WE'VE RUN SMACK INTO A HUGE ELECTRONIC FIELD THAT SHIELDS THE ENTIRE PLANET! IT'S... TRAPPED US, MR. SPOCK!

PERHAPS UNDER FULL POWER WE CAN BREAK OUT OF ITS GRIP, CAPTAIN!

LIKE SOME GREAT ENSNARED BEAST, THE ENTERPRISE STRUGGLES VIOLENTLY FOR HER FREEDOM -- BUT...

WE CAN'T BUDGE AN INCH! ANY SUGGESTIONS, MR. SPOCK?

IT'S QUITE POSSIBLE THE POWER SOURCE OF THIS FIELD IS ON THE PLANET *ITSELF* CAPTAIN! IF WE DESTROY IT-

YOUR LOGIC IS UNASSAILABLE, SPOCK! WE'LL INVESTIGATE DOWN BELOW! EXPLORATION TEAM -- STAND BY FOR ACTION! I'M GOING ALONG WITH YOU!

THEY SEEK TO DESTROY OUR SUPPLIES! *DESTROY THEM!*

AS YOU COMMAND, TARGU!

TAKE COVER! SET PHASERS TO STUN-- PERHAPS I CAN REASON WITH THEM!

SWOOSH!

WAIT! WE COME AS FRIENDS-- NOT ENEMIES! OUR SPACESHIP ORBITS YOUR PLANET AT THIS VERY MOMENT!

SPACESHIP! CEASE THE ATTACK-- WE WILL HEAR THE STRANGERS OUT!

ZAP! ZAP! ZAP!

WOOOSH!

AND AFTER KIRK HAS EXPLAINED...

YOU MUST FORGIVE OUR ASSAULT MY FRIENDS-- BUT OUR NERVES HAVE BEEN ON EDGE SINCE WE WERE *MAROONED* HERE!

MAROONED, YOU SAY!

YES, OUR FREIGHTER SPACESHIP CRASH-LANDED HERE OVER A YEAR AGO! HAD IT NOT BEEN FOR THE SUPPLIES ABOARD, WE SURELY WOULD HAVE PERISHED!

THEN, THAT EXPLAINS THE DISPENSERS WE SAW!

WELL, TARGU--YOU CAN ALL BE AT EASE! CONSIDER YOURSELVES RESCUED-- IF OUR SPACESHIP CAN EVER BREAK OUT OF THE ELECTRONIC FIELD TRAPPING IT!

ELECTRONIC FIELD? WE KNOW NOTHING ABOUT IT!

THE SOURCE MAY BE ON THE PLANET! THE SOONER WE FIND IT THE QUICKER WE'LL ALL BE OUT OF HERE! SEE YOU SOON, TARGU!

GOOD HUNTING, CAPTAIN KIRK!

THAT MUST BE ONE OF THEIR SHIPS, CAPTAIN! LET'S SEE HOW MUCH DIFFERENT THEIRS ARE FROM OURS!

ALL RIGHT, KENT, BUT LET'S MAKE IT QUICK! AFTER ALL, THAT'S NOT WHAT WE CAME FOR!

IT'S A SIMPLE ENOUGH CRAFT, ISN'T IT, CAPTAIN? I MEAN, HOW DO THEY CONTROL IT?

YES, VERY INTERESTING! LET'S RADIO A FULL DESCRIPTION TO MR. SPOCK! MAYBE HE CAN MAKE SOMETHING OF IT!

I HAVE ALL THAT INFORMATION, CAPTAIN! WE'RE RUNNING IT THROUGH THE COMPUTERS NOW! MEANWHILE WE'RE STILL WORKING ON BREAKING THE FORCE FIELD!

EXACTLY, CAPTAIN, BUT FIRST YOU MUST PROMISE TO PROTECT ME, TO TAKE ME WITH YOU WHEN YOU LEAVE!

I'LL PROMISE *NOTHING*, LARA, TILL I'VE HEARD YOUR STORY!

ALL RIGHT, I MUST TRUST YOU! I HAVE NO CHOICE! WE DID NOT CRASH-LAND HERE! WE WERE ROCKETED HERE IN ONE-WAY SPACE CRAFT! YOU SEE, WE ARE... *THE CONDEMNED!*

CONDEMNED? YOU MEAN YOU'RE *CONVICTS?* THIS PLANET IS YOUR PRISON?

EXACTLY! THE GOVERNMENT OF OUR HOME PLANET HAS DEVISED A *UNIQUE* PUNISHMENT FOR CRIMINALS!

"ONCE EACH MONTH THEY HERD ALL THOSE CONVICTED OF CRIMES TO THE ROCKETPORT WHERE THEY ARE PLACED IN MISSILES..."

"THEN, WE ARE LAUNCHED TO ONE OF THE *GLOWING* PLANETS OF THIS ASTEROID BELT..."

"FOOD, WATER AND OTHER NECESSITIES ARE SUPPLIED TO US THROUGH AUTOMATIC MACHINES WHICH YOU HAVE ALREADY SEEN, SO WE SURVIVE UNTIL THE SENTENCE IS CARRIED OUT..."

SOUNDS LIKE A PRETTY PROGRESSIVE PENAL SYSTEM! HOW LONG MUST YOU REMAIN HERE?

PROGRESSIVE? IT'S SADISTIC! I TOLD YOU, CAPTAIN, WE ARE CONDEMNED! WE ARE HERE AWAITING *EXECUTION!*

EXECUTED? BUT WHEN AND HOW IS THE DEATH PENALTY CARRIED OUT?

WHEN? THAT'S THE HORROR OF IT! WE DON'T *KNOW* WHEN!

LOOK AT THAT WEASEL, LARA! TRYING TO SAVE HIS MISERABLE NECK, I'LL BET!

YEAH, BY RUINING *OUR* CHANCE TO ESCAPE!

ROUND UP THE OTHERS! BUT STAY UNDER COVER! DON'T ATTACK UNLESS I GIVE THE WORD! MAYBE I CAN STILL *TALK* OUR WAY OUT OF THIS!

SEE IF YOU CAN REACH THE CAPTAIN, LIEUTENANT! THERE'S NO FURTHER NEED FOR HIM TO STAY BELOW!

MR. SPOCK! COME HERE *QUICKLY!* LOOK AT THIS!

AS SOON AS WE BLASTED HOLES IN THE FORCE FIELD, WE GOT A READING ON THE INFRA-RED SEISMOGRAPH! LOOK AT THAT NEEDLE *JUMP!*

FIND OUT WHAT'S CAUSING IT! THAT'S A *CRITICAL* READING!

KIRK TO ENTERPRISE! DO YOU READ ME?

LOUD AND CLEAR, CAPTAIN! WE'VE BROKEN THROUGH THE ELECTRONIC TRAP! WE'RE THROUGH!

AND CAPTAIN, WE'RE GETTING A CRITICAL READING ON THE SEISMOGRAPH! DO YOU FEEL TREMORS DOWN THERE?

NEVER MIND THAT NOW! BEAM US ABOARD-- IMMEDI-ATELY!

STAND BY TO BEAM EXPLORATION PARTY ABOARD, ON MY COMMAND! READY...

YOU AND YOUR MURDEROUS HENCHMEN ABOARD THE ENTERPRISE, TARGU? NEVER! WE'RE A FULLY EQUIPPED FIGHTING SPACESHIP! YOU CAN'T HOLD US FOREVER!

WE CAN TRY!

WHAT ARE WE GOING TO DO, MR. SPOCK?

ONE THING WE **WON'T** DO IS PANIC! A LITTLE LOGIC WILL SOLVE THIS PROBLEM! LET'S CONSIDER THE POSSIBILITIES!

THE CAPTAIN IS THEIR INSURANCE! THEY DON'T DARE HARM--

MR. SPOCK! I'VE FOUND THE CAUSE OF THE SEISMOGRAPH READING! IT'S...IT'S...

AND IT IS THEN THAT MR. SPOCK SENDS THROUGH A SHOCKING REPORT FROM THE ENTERPRISE...

CAPTAIN KIRK! I-I'VE FOUND THE PROBLEM ON YOUR PRISON PLANET! ITS HEART IS A MOLTEN BALL OF FIRE!

...AN INTERNAL VOLCANO THAT WILL BLOW THE PLANET INTO A *SUPER NOVA* WITHIN *TWENTY-FOUR HOURS!*

END PART I

STAR TREK

The Secret of... EXECUTION ASTEROID

PART II

CAPTAIN'S LOG, STAR DATE 19:04.5 -- WE ARE IN A DESPERATE PLIGHT! MR. SPOCK HAS JUST INFORMED US THAT THE CRIMINAL ASTEROID WE ARE UPON IS DUE TO EXPLODE WITHIN 24 HOURS... AND THERE IS NO CHANCE OF ESCAPE WITHOUT ENDANGERING THE ENTERPRISE AND HER MISSION...

TH-THE ASTEROID IS GOING TO *EXPLODE!* ARE YOU *SURE*, MR. SPOCK?

POSITIVE, CAPTAIN KIRK!

SO...THE SECRET OF ASTEROID X IS OUT, EH, KIRK!

SO *THAT'S* HOW YOU GALAXY KILLERS ARE EXECUTED...BY EXPLODING ASTEROIDS?

EXACTLY! A MOST UNIQUE MANNER OF CAPITAL PUNISHMENT, IS IT NOT?

YOU SEE, IT HAS THE ADDED BEAUTY OF MENTAL TORTURE... FOR NONE KNOW JUST WHEN THE SUPER NOVA EFFECT WILL TAKE PLACE...

ONLY YOUR INGENIOUS MR. SPOCK HAS LEARNED *THAT!*

AS LARA, THE BETRAYER, INFORMED YOU -- WE CRIMINALS ARE LAUNCHED TO THE *DEATH ASTEROIDS* BY ROCKET...

"EACH MONTH THE CONDEMNED LEAVE THE HOME PLANET FOREVER IN ONE-WAY MISSILES..."

WHICH ASTEROID DO YOU THINK WE'LL LAND ON, TARGU?

WHAT DIFFER-ENCE DOES IT MAKE? THEY'RE ALL ALIKE!

EXCEPT FOR *ONE* THING... THEY DON'T ALL BLOW UP AT THE *SAME TIME!*

"NOT EVERYBODY LOOKS AT HIS NEW LIFE THE SAME WAY. SOME ARE WEAK AND GIVE UP ALL HOPE, OTHERS ARE STRONG..."

HOW LONG DO WE HAVE, TARGU? A WEEK...A MONTH?

MAYBE WE HAVE MANY YEARS! AND I INTEND TO MAKE THE MOST OF *EVERY* MINUTE!

MOVE THAT FOOD DISPENSER OVER HERE WHERE WE CAN PROTECT IT! AND THEN GET THE DISPENSERS OUT OF THE OTHER SHIPS!

I'M ENTITLED TO MY RATIONS THE SAME AS EVERY-BODY ELSE!

YOU'LL GET RATIONS WHEN TARGU SAYS SO! IF YOU WANT TO *EAT*, YOU'LL *WORK* FOR TARGU!

"IN TIME WE DISMANTLED THE ROCKETS THAT BROUGHT US HERE AND MADE HALFWAY DECENT LIVING QUARTERS..."

IT ISN'T RIGHT, TARGU'S NO BETTER THAN THE *REST* OF US!

IF YOU WANT TO FIGHT IT OUT WITH THOSE *KILLERS* OF HIS, GO AHEAD! I'LL DO AS HE SAYS AND TAKE *WHAT* HE GIVES ME!

YES, CAPTAIN, I MADE THE PEOPLE ON THIS PLANET-- ALL MURDERERS, THIEVES AND TOUGHS-- RESPECT ME, FEAR ME, OBEY ME! TARGU *ALWAYS* MAKES OUT! TARGU *ALWAYS* SURVIVES!

I'M GLAD TO KNOW THE KIND OF CREATURE I'M DEALING WITH!

WELL, I GUESS IT *IS* OUR TURN NOW! GIVE ME THAT BLASTED RADIO OF YOURS, KIRK!

MR. SPOCK, THIS IS TARGU, THE *BIG BOSS* OF ASTEROID X! HEED MY WORDS WELL, GENIUS MAN OF THE ENTERPRISE!

YOUR CAPTAIN KIRK WILL BE JUST AS DEAD AS *WE* WILL IF YOU DON'T TELEPORT MY MEN TO YOUR SHIP WITH YOUR OWN!

NOT EVERYBODY, SPOCK, JUST ME AND MY LOYAL, TRUSTED MEN! ANSWER ME, SPOCK!

I TAKE MY ORDERS FROM MY CAPTAIN, *NOT* FROM YOU, TARGU! LET ME SPEAK WITH HIM!

HE WANTS TO TALK WITH YOU! I'LL GIVE YOU THIRTY SECONDS! REMEMBER, YOUR LIFE DEPENDS ON IT!

BRING ONLY A HANDFUL OF HIS MEN ABOARD, IN EXCHANGE FOR YOUR SAFETY! IT SEEMS LIKE AN ACCEPTABLE BARGAIN!

NO!

THIS CHARACTER IS *DEADLY!* AND CLEVER! I'M AT HIS MERCY NOW! AND HE ISN'T GOING TO TURN ME LOOSE ON BOARD THE ENTERPRISE! HE'LL HOLD A KNIFE AT MY *THROAT* EVERY SECOND!

BUT HE LEAVES US NO *OTHER* CHOICE, CAPTAIN!

YES, HE DOES, SPOCK-- *ONE* OTHER CHOICE! YOU'RE TO TAKE COMMAND OF THE ENTERPRISE AND TAKE HER AWAY FROM THIS POWDER KEG OF AN ASTEROID AS FAST AS YOU CAN! THAT'S AN *ORDER*, MR. SPOCK!

YOU WON'T DO IT, SPOCK! YOU *CAN'T* LEAVE THE CAPTAIN DOWN THERE--

SURELY, THERE MUST BE SOME WAY--

YOU *HEARD* THE CAPTAIN'S *ORDER*, GENTLEMEN!

ON THE OTHER HAND, YOU *ALSO* HEARD THE CAPTAIN GIVE ME COMMAND OF THE SHIP *PRIOR* TO THAT! SO TECHNICALLY, I AM *NOT* BOUND BY THAT ORDER!

SPOCK, YOUR VULCAN LOGIC WINS AGAIN!

HOWEVER, WE STILL HAVE TO RESCUE THE CAPTAIN WITHOUT BRINGING THOSE ALIEN MURDERERS ABOARD! AND WE DON'T HAVE MUCH TIME!

SHADES OF PLUTO! I THINK I HAVE THE ANSWER!

QUICKLY, SCOTTY, INTO DAMAGE CONTROL! WE HAVE *WORK* TO DO!

GET THOSE METAL SECTIONS DOWN! HAVE YOUR MEN READY FOR SOME SUPER-FAST *CONSTRUCTION* WORK! I'LL BE BACK IN A MINUTE!

THAT I WILL, MR. SPOCK... WHATEVER YOUR PLAN MIGHT BE!

THROUGH THE NIGHT, THE ENTERPRISE TEAM AWAIT THEIR EXPLOSIVE FATE...

WHAT A SORRY WAY TO GO -- TRAPPED WITH KILLERS ON A DOOMED ASTEROID!

NOTHING, FOSTER, NOT EVEN OUR LIVES MUST JEOPARDIZE THE ENTERPRISE AND HER MISSION...

THAT'S THE IMPORTANT THING -- FOR OUR SHIP OF THE STAR FLEET TO CONTINUE SEARCHING THE UNKNOWN AND UNLOCK ITS MYSTERIES!

53

THEN, AS THE BOSS CONVICT APPROACHES THE DESCENDING CRAFT...

LOOK OUT! THE GALAXY PRISONER ROCKET HAS GONE WILD! IT IS NOT LANDING IN THE REGULAR FASHION!

PRISONER HUTS ARE SMASHED APART AS THE ROCKET CAREENS DOWN FOR A LANDING...

CRAAAASH!

FINALLY, IT SKIDS TO A HALT...

ALL RIGHT, MEN! LET'S GET THOSE DISPENSERS! MAYBE WE CAN EAT OURSELVES TO DEATH BEFORE THIS ASTEROID BLOWS!

SCRREECH!

But as the rocket port swings open...

Targu! Th-they are not galaxy prisoners!

Scotty! Spock's sent a raiding party down to help us!

It's a trick! Get back to our prisoners before it's too late!

But it is already too late...

Stand fast! Wait for Scotty to reach us!

Abruptly, Mr. Spock's voice crackles over Captain Kirk's radio...

Captain! Is Mr. Scott's raiding party succeeding?

Affirmative! He's isolating the convicts with those fire bombs!

Hurry, sir! Tell Spock to beam us aboard! That fire wall won't last long!

WE ARE *CLEAR*, MR. SPOCK! BUT CONVICTS ARE APPROACHING THROUGH A BREAK IN THE FIRE WALL!

I AM THROWING TELEPORTATION SWITCH NOW, CAPTAIN!

INSTANTLY, THE FIGURES BEGIN TO DISAPPEAR FROM THE DOOMED ASTEROID...

AND MOMENTS LATER THEIR BODIES TAKE FORM IN THE TELEPORTATION CHAMBER OF THE ENTERPRISE...

ALL ROCKETS ON FULL!

WHEN YOU INSPECTED THAT ROCKET YOU FOUND, JIM, I NEVER DREAMED HOW *VALUABLE* THAT INFORMATION--

SPOCK! YOU RISKED THIS SHIP AND THE LIVES OF *EVERY* MAN ABOARD!

AS A MAN, I COULD FORGET THAT! BUT AS AN OFFICER, I *CAN'T* FORGET YOU DISOBEYED A DIRECT *ORDER*!

OH, BUT I DIDN'T, JIM, AS DR. McCOY AND MR. SCOTT WILL EXPLAIN!

In fact, Jim, I enjoy being captain so much, I may never turn back command to you! But it's all academic if we don't get out of range fast!

For long seconds she streaks into space! And far below, the prisoner planet suddenly bursts asunder...

The asteroid has blown! Hold tight, men! We're still within her concussion range!

The violent force of the exploding planet rocks the Enterprise like a ship in a storm-tossed sea...

Our good ship is getting the test of her life, Captain! Let us hope her hull holds!

And finally...

We are clear! Outside of a few thousand asteroid pieces in our hull I cannot see any signs of serious damage!

(Whew!) Good show, Mr. Spock! That was the squeeze play of our lives!

The Devil's Isle of space--nothing but a floating cloud of dust now! It seems brutal to have left those people there...

Execution by asteroid explosion is the way of their society! We had no other choice but to leave them, Captain!

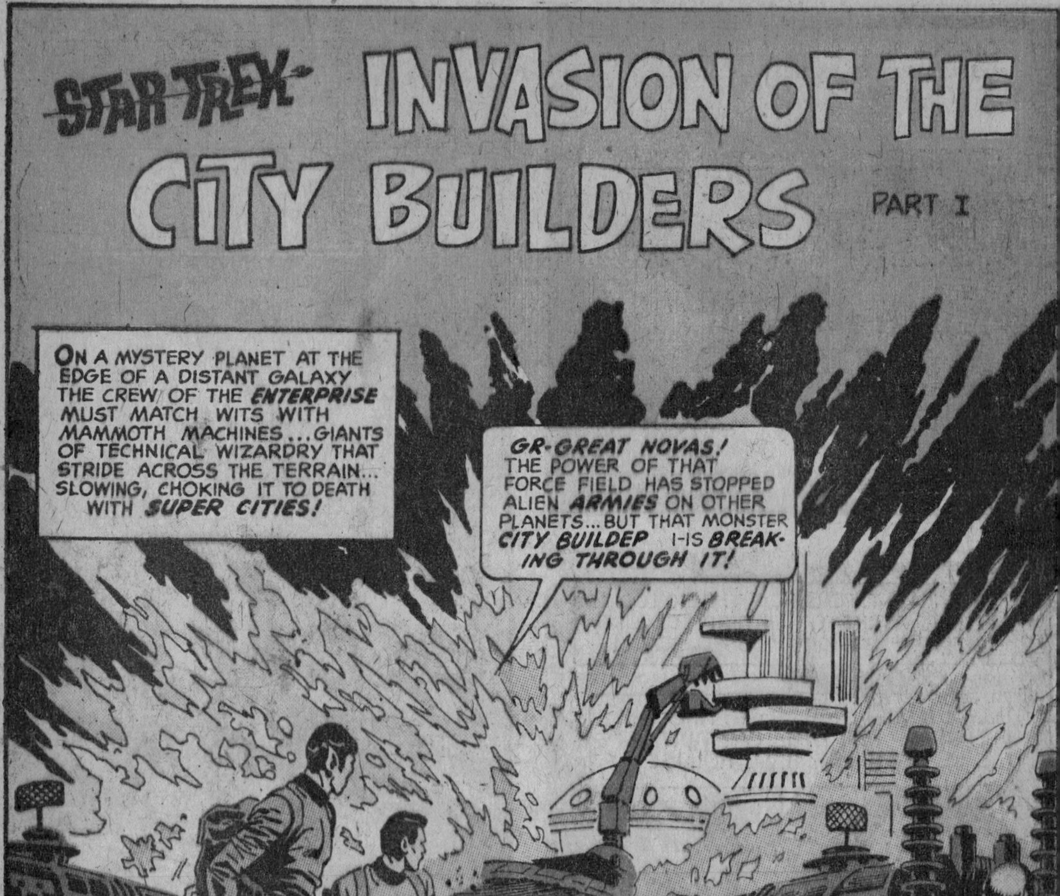

Captain's Log, Stardate 20:14.6 . . . . DATA REF. . . .3.00-3.26

CAPTAIN'S LOG, STAR DATE 20:14.6 -- MISSION HAS BEEN DELAYED BY DIRECT METEORITE HIT ON ROCKET ENGINE #4 -- REPAIRS BEING MADE -- EXPECT TO CONTINUE TOWARD OBJECTIVE SHORTLY...

FUEL LINE WELDED OKAY, CAPTAIN KIRK! WE ARE RETURNING TO THE SHIP!

ROGER! GOOD SHOW -- AND WATCH YOUR FOOTING ON THE WAY HOME!

WE'RE ON COURSE AT FULL SPEED AGAIN, MR. SPOCK! NOW LET'S CONTINUE WITH OUR RESEARCH ON ALPHA Z-21 -- PLANET QUESTIONMARK!

I'LL INSERT THE FILMED PLANETARY HISTORY FILE!

ONE HUNDRED YEARS AGO A DEEP GALAXY SHIP MANAGED TO SEND THESE RADIO FILMS BACK TO A MOTHER SHIP BEFORE APPARENTLY EXPLODING!

THEN, AS THE RADIO-PHOTO FILMS TAKEN A CENTURY BEFORE FLOOD A PICTURE ON THE SCREEN...

EVIDENTLY THE SPACE-SHIP WAS RECONNOITER-ING THE PLANET AT LOW ALTITUDE AND USED A TELE-SCOPIC CAMERA!

A BANK OF ULTRA-MODERN MACHINES..

THEY APPEAR TO BE WORKING TOGETHER IN SOME SORT OF A MECHANICAL COMPLEX!

THE CITIZENS! OBVIOUSLY THEY'RE OF A HIGH CIVILI-ZATION...BEING WAITED ON BY MACHINES!

YES-S, MR. SPOCK! IT LOOKS AS IF THEY BELIEVE IN A LIFE OF COMFORT!

STRANGE! THERE WEREN'T ANY CITIZENS SEEN ABOUT THAT MAMMOTH MACHINE COMPLEX...NO WORKERS!

THE PICTURE'S FADING, CAPTAIN! WE CAME INTO POSSESSION OF ONLY A FEW SECONDS OF FILM!

CAPTAIN TO CONTROL! WHAT IS OUR ESTIMATED ARRIVAL TIME AT ALPHA Z-21?

TWO LUNAR HOURS ONE GALAXY MINUTE, SIR!

AND EXACTLY TWO LUNAR HOURS LATER, AS THE PAIR LOOKS THROUGH TELESCOPIC VIEW SCANNER...

THERE SHE IS--A MYSTERY PLANET IN THE GALAXY FOR CENTURIES!

OXYGEN READING HIGH, CAPTAIN! THE ATMOSPHERE IS FULL OF IT! THERE ARE INDICATIONS OF WATER...

ROGER, MR. SPOCK!

CUT SPEED AND BRING HER DOWN, CONTROL!

...AND ALSO LARGE MASSES OF METALLIC MATTER OVER THE PLANET!

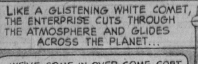

LIKE A GLISTENING WHITE COMET, THE ENTERPRISE CUTS THROUGH THE ATMOSPHERE AND GLIDES ACROSS THE PLANET...

WE'VE COME IN OVER SOME SORT OF SUPER-CITY! CAN YOU MAKE OUT ANY LIFE, MR. SPOCK?

NOTHING, CAPTAIN!

FOR A HUNDRED MILES, THE REMARKABLE EXPLORATION CRAFT SOARS OVER THE ALIEN TERRAIN AND...

INCREASE SPEED!

MILE AFTER MILE OF URBAN COMPLEX WITHOUT SIGN OF LIFE!

BUT STILL ANOTHER NINE HUNDRED MILES LATER

BUILDING AFTER BUILDING, STREET AFTER STREET... EMPTY, BARREN! WHAT DO YOU MAKE OF IT, MR. SPOCK?

UTTER BEWILDERMENT! THERE ARE NO SIGNS OF A CATASTROPHE, THE STRUCTURES SHOW NO DECAY! MOST PERPLEXING!

FINALLY, AS THE ENTERPRISE ROCKETS AHEAD AT INCREASED SPEED...

OPEN AREA AHEAD! THAT'S WHERE OUR TELEPORTATION TEAM CAN LAND! TAKE HER INTO ORBIT AND PREPARE TELEPORT CHAMBER!

ROGER, CAPTAIN!

HER GARGANTUAN ROCKETS WHIP THE ENTERPRISE INTO ORBIT FAR ABOVE PLANET QUESTIONMARK...

MR. SPOCK, YOU'D BETTER JOIN US ON THE EXPLORATION TEAM! YOUR TECHNICAL SERVICES MAY BE NEEDED TO UNRAVEL OUR MYSTERY!

READY TO GO, CAPTAIN!

MOMENTS LATER, BEAMS IN THE TELEPORTATION CHAMBER ILLUMINATE THE EXPLORATION TEAM...

AND A MICRO-SECOND AFTERWARD, THE FIGURES MATERIALIZE ON ALPHA Z-21...

(WHEW-W-W!) WHY, THE SUPER-CITY ENDS ABRUPTLY... AS IF IT HAD BEEN CUT OFF WITH A KNIFE BEFORE IT WAS COMPLETE!

OUR FIRST OPERATION SHOULD BE TO SEARCH FOR SIGNS OF LIFE WITHIN THOSE BIZARRE BUILDINGS!

BUT AS CAPTAIN KIRK GIVES INSTRUCTIONS TO HIS MEN, HE CAN NOT KNOW THAT THE LIFE HE SEEKS HAS ALREADY FOUND HIM...

ALIEN VISITORS! WHAT SHALL WE DO NOW, OH, GREAT LEADER, KRILL?

FRIENDS OR ENEMIES, THEY MUST AWAIT OUR ATTENTION! PLANS CAN NOT BE CHANGED NOW!

AND SUDDENLY, AS THE WORDS HAVE BARELY LEFT KRILL'S MOUTH...

IT COMES!

RUMBLE!

WHILE AT THE ENTERPRISE LANDING CREW SITE...

T-THE GROUND SHAKING! EARTHQUAKE!

NO! IT IS SOME SORT OF SURFACE DISTURBANCE!

THEN...

MR. SPOCK! OVER THERE--IT LOOKS LIKE A PARADE OF HEAVY EQUIPMENT!

YES! THAT'S WHAT IS CREATING THE DISTURBANCE!

A FEW MINUTES LATER, THE MEN OF THE ENTERPRISE GAPE IN AWE AS...

WHY, THEY'RE CREATING BUILDINGS, ROADS-- EXTENDING THE CITY!

BUT THOSE MACHINES--THERE'S NOBODY OPERATING THEM! IT'S POSITIVELY EERIE!

A BEAM OF SUPER-INTENSIFIED LIGHT STREAKS INTO THE MACHINE'S INNARDS AND...

YOU *HAVE!* THE MACHINE HAS STOPPED BUILDING! IT'S *WITHDRAWING!* AND ALL THE OTHER MACHINERY WITH IT! AMAZING!

BUT WHAT HAPPENED TO THE PEOPLE?

I THINK YOU HAVE SHORT-CIRCUITED IT, CAPTAIN!

THERE!

TENSELY, CAUTIOUSLY, THE ALIENS COME INTO THE OPEN... AND AS KIRK SPEAKS IN THE INTERPLANETARY LANGUAGE ESPERANTA...

THEY'RE AFRAID OF US...

WE ARE FRIENDS! WE ONLY COME TO AID YOU!

THANK YOU, VISITORS FROM ANOTHER WORLD! WE OWE YOU A GREAT DEBT!

YOU OWE US NOTHING, SIR-- EXCEPT PERHAPS AN EXPLANATION TO YOUR MONSTROUS PROBLEM HERE!

YOU COULD NOT *DESTROY* THE MONSTER CITY MAKER-- BUT YOU HAVE FORCED IT TO GO BACK FOR REPAIRS!

PLEASE,,,TELL US WHO YOU ARE...AND HOW THAT FANTASTIC MACHINE CAME TO BE!

IT IS A LONG AND SHAMEFUL STORY! I AM KRILL-- LEADER OF ALL WHO REMAIN OF THE CIVILIZATION ON THE PLANET ZARTA!

150 YEARS AGO WE WERE A PROUD AND PROSPEROUS RACE OF MANY MILLIONS! TODAY, A DOZEN OF THOSE MECHANICAL DEMONS RULE THE PLANET AND THREATEN MY VILLAGE IN THE MOUNTAINS YONDER!

"IT FIRST BEGAN WHEN OUR SUPER-CIVILIZATION BEGAN EXPERIMENTING WITH MACHINES TO TAKE OVER OUR EVERYDAY CHORES..."

LETTER... FOR... URGO FAMILY!

"AS THE YEARS PASSED, OUR BRILLIANT MEN OF SCIENCE CREATED MORE AND MORE INGENIOUS MACHINES... ELECTRONIC TEAMS HARVESTED OUR CROPS, PROCESSED, PACKAGED AND DELIVERED THEM..."

"SOON, OUR MASTER DEVICES SPREAD THROUGHOUT OUR ENTIRE CULTURE! OUR POLICE FORCES BECAME FULLY AUTOMATED THOUGH THERE WAS HARDLY ANY CRIME..."

"THE WORLD OF BUSINESS WAS NEXT... COMPUTERS MADE OUR DECISIONS ON THE STOCK MARKET..."

BUY! SELL! SELL! BUY!

"FINALLY, THEY ENTERED THE SACRED SANCTUM OF THE VERY SCIENCE THAT HAD CREATED THEM..."

LOOK AT THIS BLUEPRINT OUR MASTER PLANNING MACHINE HAS CONCEIVED! A SYSTEM OF CO-ORDINATED SELF-OPERATING MACHINERY FOR BUILDING ENTIRE CITIES!

AH, YES...WE WERE LIVING IN UTOPIA! OUR NECESSITIES WERE ALL PROVIDED FOR US! BUSINESS AND COMMERCE WERE SYSTEMATIZED AND CARRIED OUT BY OUR KNOWLEDGE PROCESSING MACHINES, FAR MORE ASTUTE THAN HUMAN MINDS!

"OUR LEADERS SMUGLY WATCHED AS OUR AUTOMATED FACTORY CREATED THE MOST COMPLEX MACHINERY OF ALL--*THE CITY BUILDER!*"

A GREAT TRIUMPH! SOON *ALL* FORMS OF LABOR WILL BE ELIMINATED!

THERE'S NO END TO WHAT OUR MACHINES CAN ACHIEVE!

"IN LESS THAN A MOON MONTH IT WAS FINISHED-- AND IT FULFILLED OUR HIGHEST EXPECTATIONS... "

NO HUMAN HAND COULD CONSTRUCT A CITY SO PERFECT...SO SYMMETRICAL IN EVERY DETAIL!

BUT REMEMBER, IT TOOK *MAN* TO CREATE THE MACHINES WHICH CREATED THE MACHINE WHICH BUILT THE CITY!

"THEN IT BEGAN...THE FIRST NOTE IN WHAT WAS SOON TO BE A MELODY OF DOOM FOR THE PLANET ZARTA..."

TH-THE CITY BUILDER! I-IT HAS GONE BERSERK... THE MACHINE IS DIGGING INTO THE MOUNTAINSIDE!

KAZAR! HOW CAN THIS BE?

SEE THERE! T-THE SUPER REFRIGERATION UNIT WE BUILT INTO OUR CITY BUILDER IS COOLING THE MOLTEN GIRDERS I-IN *SECONDS!*

A WHOLE NEW CITY? *WHY?* THIS MACHINERY IS SUPPOSED TO BUILD ONLY ACCORDING TO NEED!

IT WILL HAVE TO STOP WHEN IT RUNS OUT OF MATERIALS!

"BUT OUR AUTOMATED POLICE WERE POWERLESS! THEY HAD BEEN BUILT TO DEAL WITH HUMAN CRIMINALS, NOT WITH HEAVY MACHINERY!"

THE CITY-BUILDERS WERE MADE TO WITH-STAND *ANY* ABUSE! OUR *OWN* MACHINES HAVE DEFEATED US!

THAT ALL HAPPENED OVER A HUNDRED YEARS AGO! IN A FEW YEARS OUR HEAVY EQUIPMENT MANUFACTURING PLANT PRODUCED TWO MORE OF THE GREAT CITY-BUILDING TEAMS!

AND SO THE PACE OF OUR CITY BUILDING ACCELERATED! WE HAD PLANTED THE IDEA OF EFFICIENCY INTO OUR ELECTRONIC BRAINS, BUT NO CONCERN FOR HUMAN NEEDS!

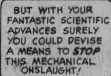

BUT WITH YOUR FANTASTIC SCIENTIFIC ADVANCES SURELY YOU COULD DEVISE A MEANS TO *STOP* THIS MECHANICAL ONSLAUGHT!

CAPTAIN KIRK, MACHINES HAD BEEN DESIGNING, PROGRAMMING AND PRODUCING MACHINES FOR YEARS! MAN NO LONGER UNDERSTOOD THEM!

BUT ACTUALLY, IT WAS THIS *TINY LITTLE GEAR* THAT REALLY SOUNDED THE DEATH KNELL FOR ZARTA!

YOU SEE, AFTER YEARS OF AUTOMATED PAMPERING OUR PEOPLES WERE LIKE CHILDREN BEING FED IN A CRIB! WHEN THIS ONE SMALL GEAR BROKE DOWN WE BEGAN TO STARVE...

THIS WAS OUR MASTER AGRICULTURAL UNIT! WITHOUT IT, OUR FOOD COULD NOT BE HARVESTED, PROCESSED, PACKED, OR DISTRIBUTED!

AND IT COULD NOT BE REPLACED!... FOR ITS SECRET HAD BEEN LOST!

WHY DIDN'T THE PEOPLE GO *BACK* TO THE FIELDS! THEY COULD FEED THEMSELVES AS THEY DID BEFORE -- IN THE *OLD-FASHIONED* MANNER!

WE NOT ONLY DID NO PHYSICAL LABOR, WE COULD NO LONGER EVEN THINK, PLAN, LOOK AHEAD, MAKE DECISIONS! MAN WAS *OBSOLETE!*

OF COURSE! IT WOULD TAKE TIME...ANOTHER GENERATION, PERHAPS, TO RELEARN THINGS! KRILL...THE CREW OF THE ENTERPRISE WILL TRY TO HELP YOU!

IT'S NO USE, CAPTAIN KIRK! SOON *EVERY SQUARE INCH* OF ZARTA WILL BE COVERED WITH GLEAMING CITIES—AND THERE WON'T BE A SOUL LEFT TO LIVE IN THEM!

CONTINUED...

STAR TREK · The BRIDGE TO CATASTROPHE

PART II

ON ZARTA, THE MYSTERY WORLD REFERRED TO AS *PLANET QUESTIONMARK*, THE CREW OF THE ENTERPRISE JOIN FORCES WITH THE LAST OF AN ALIEN CIVILIZATION TO STOP THE TERRIBLE *"PROGRESS"* OF... *THE CITY BUILDERS!*

THEY COME -- *THREE* OF THEM! THERE ARE ONLY TEN THOUSAND ACRES OF OF OPEN LAND LEFT ...IF THEY BUILD ON THAT, OUR PLANET IS FINISHED!

SIT TIGHT, KRILL! WE'LL WORK *SOMETHING* OUT!

THEN, KRILL'S MEN SWARM OUT OF HIDING...

KRILL! WHAT SHALL WE DO? THE IRON ONES COME AGAIN!

DO NOT FEAR, ZIKA--OUR ALIEN FRIENDS ARE HERE TO HELP US! OUR VISITORS COME FROM A GREAT SPACE-SHIP CALLED *ENTERPRISE!* THEY... UNDERSTAND OUR PROBLEM!

WE'LL HAVE A SOCIAL *LATER*, GENTLEMEN! RIGHT NOW, THOSE MACHINES HAVE TO BE DEALT WITH...

WHAT DO YOU THINK, MR. SPOCK? CAN WE DO ANYTHING TO STOP THEM FROM CONTINUING THE CITY COMPLEX ONWARD?

THEIR VIBRATIONS REGISTER THAT THEY WEIGH OVER A THOUSAND TONS, CAPTAIN...

IF WE MADE A TRENCH WITH OUR EARTH DIS-INTEGRATORS IN THEIR PATH WE MIGHT MOUSE-TRAP THEM! WITH SUCH WEIGHT THEY MAY BECOME BOGGED DOWN...

QUICKLY, THE "SOIL DESTROYERS" ARE BROUGHT INTO PLAY...

HURRY! THOSE GAR-GANTUAN GADGETS ARE HEADING FOR THE EDGE OF THE CITY COMPLEX LIKE MOTHS TO A CANDLE!

WE'RE DOWN A HUNDRED FEET -- THAT SHOULD DO IT!

ZZZZZZ

IT HAS SUCCEEDED JUST AS THE CITY-BUILDERS BEGAN TO BUILD THEY HAVE TUMBLED INTO THE ALIEN-MADE PIT! YOUR FRIENDS ARE WISE, OH KRILL!

HOLD UP! THE SHOW ISN'T OVER *YET!*

CLOSER...CLOSER THE IRON STRUCTURE-MAKING CREATURE COME... UNTIL...

FOR A MOMENT ALL IS STILL... THEN THE MACHINES THUMP INTO ACTION ONCE AGAIN...

SPOCK!

TH-THEY ARE BUILDING STRUCTURES *BENEATH* THEM, RAISING THEMSELVES OUT OF YOUR PIT! WH-WHAT SHALL WE DO NOW, CAPTAIN KIRK?

MY PEOPLE—THEY ARE TURNING TO THE ALIENS FOR GUIDANCE NOW! THEY IGNORE ME!

A FORCE FIELD, MR. SPOCK! IT MAY WORK!

AND SHORTLY, AS THE MASTERS OF CEMENT AND STEEL CLIMB OUT OF THE TRENCH ATOP THEIR OWN CONSTRUCTION WORK...

HERE THEY COME! THE POWER OF THAT FORCE FIELD HAS STOPPED ARMIES... IT SHOULD JOLT THOSE METAL MONSTERS SOME!

PERHAPS! BUT THEY ARE OF A METAL UNKNOWN TO US, CAPTAIN!

A BLAZING BLAST OF LIGHT ERUPTS AS THE CITY BUILDERS THUNDER INTO THE FORCE FIELD...

THEY'RE CAUGHT GOOD AND SQUARE!

BUT LOOK--THEY'RE *STILL* BUILDING STRUCTURES!

IT'S *GOT* TO HOLD ...IT *MUST!*

SPUTTER WHOOOOSH

THEN...

FANTASTIC! THE FORCE FIELD ISN'T POWERFUL ENOUGH! THEY'LL BE COMING TO A BIG RIVER SOON! SURELY THAT WILL STOP THEM!

NO! NO!

YOU MEAN THOSE HEAVY MACHINES CAN CROSS RIVERS THIS SIZE? BUT HOW?

THEY HAVE THE CONCENTRATED INTELLIGENCE OF A THOUSAND ENGINEERS WITHIN THEM!

EVERY OBSTACLE THEY FACE BECOMES A SIMPLE EXERCISE IN PROBLEM SOLVING! YOU SAW HOW THEY OVERCAME YOUR DITCH! WATCH WHEN THEY REACH THE WATER'S EDGE!

THEY HAVE IDENTIFIED THE PROBLEM! NOW THEY ARE ANALYZING IT AND DECIDING WHAT ACTION TO TAKE!

SWIFTLY, THE MACHINES SWING INTO ACTION. WITHIN HALF AN HOUR THEIR SOLUTION BECOMES OBVIOUS...

OF COURSE! THEY'RE BUILDING A BRIDGE!

SO LOGICAL, SO SIMPLE! BUT STILL, CAPTAIN, MOST REMARKABLE!

INCREDIBLE! NOW THE MACHINE WILL SINK ANOTHER TOWER IN MID-RIVER, AND THEN--

WE MUST ATTACK IT AGAIN, BEFORE IT GETS ACROSS!

WE *HAVE* ATTACKED, KRILL, AND *FAILED!* WE MUST BE AS LOGICAL, AS ANALYTICAL AS THEY ARE!

MEANING YOU INTEND TO DO *NOTHING!*

THERE IS *ONE* POSSIBILITY, CAPTAIN --WE MUST FIND A WEAKNESS IN THEIR MIRACLE METAL!

SPOCK TO ENTER-PRISE: TELEPORT AT ONCE METALLIC TEST KIT! OUR CO-ORDINATES ARE...

WITHIN MINUTES, THE REQUESTED EQUIPMENT MATERIALIZES...

CAN YOU REALLY FIND A FLAW IN THE METAL, MR. SPOCK?

THOUGH I'M NOT FAMILIAR WITH ALL SUBSTANCES IN THE UNIVERSE, LOGIC TELLS ME EVERY SUBSTANCE CAN BEEN BROKEN DOWN BY *SOME* PROCESS!

WHICH MAY TAKE *YEARS* TO DISCOVER!

KRILL IS RIGHT! THESE ARE *HIS* PEOPLE! THIS IS *HIS* JOB!

OF COURSE!

WE HAVE A WEAPON NOW KRILL! BUT WE NEED *YOU* TO OPERATE IT! YOU KNOW THESE CUNNING MACHINES BETTER THAN WE DO! WILL YOU COME WITH US?

NO!

NO? YOU MEAN YOU'LL STAND BY AND *LET* YOUR PEOPLE BE DESTROYED?

I MEAN I'LL DO IT-- *ALONE!*

ALONE? THAT'S SUICIDE?

ALONE I HELD THESE PEOPLE TOGETHER! *WITHOUT* ME THEY WOULD HAVE PERISHED YEARS AGO! I ALONE CAN SAVE THEM NOW!

WHY THAT EGOMANIAC! HE'S MORE CONCERNED WITH KEEPING HIS POWER THAN SAVING HIS PEOPLE!

HE'S VERY MUCH LIKE YOU *EARTH* PEOPLE IN THAT RESPECT, CAPTAIN!

AS KRILL MOVES IN ON THE BRIDGE...

OUR ACID SOLUTION WORKED IN THE TEST! NOW WE'LL SEE HOW IT WORKS IN *ACTION!*

IT'S *SUCCEEDING!* THE METAL IS BEGINNING TO MELT! MUST KEEP SPRAYING!

BUT ABOVE, THE GIANT MACHINE SENSES THAT SOMETHING IS WRONG-- AND REACTS...

RED-HOT RIVETS! THE BUILDER KNOWS I'M HERE!

THE BRIDGE ITSELF WILL SHELTER ME FROM THE RIVETS! BUT WHEN IT FAILS, CAN I GET AWAY?

THAT *DID* IT! IT'S COMING *DOWN!*

That was much too close! The others will be easier!

CRRRACK

And after all the city builders have been destroyed...

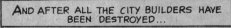

Well, I guess the hardest part is over!

Yes, thanks to you and your men, Captain Kirk! Now we can destroy the factories which *produce* the machines!

And we still have to demolish *so much* of our useless cities and reclaim the land!

And as the men are beamed back to the Enterprise...

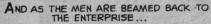

It will take us generations! But we *can* and *will* do it! Good-bye, Captain!

Star Fleet Command is pleased with our report, Mr. Spock!

Naturally, Captain! We preserved a civilization which would otherwise have perished! It is the *only logical* reaction!

STAR TREK · THE PERIL OF PLANET QUICK CHANGE
PART I — THE CREATURES OF LIGHT

SPOCK! I'VE HAD ENOUGH OF YOUR MUMBO JUMBO THEORIES! LOOK AT THAT—TREES SPROUTING FROM SAND...MOUNTAINS RISING! NOBODY OR ANYTHING CAN CALM THIS PLANET DOWN! I'M ORDERING AN IMMEDIATE TELE-PORTATION BACK TO THE ENTERPRISE!

IT WAS A WORLD IN DEEP SPACE THAT EVEN THE GALAXY-WISE CREW OF THE *ENTERPRISE* HAD NEVER DREAMED OF--A PLANET THAT CONVULSED, SPROUTED FOLIAGE, MOUNTAINS AND WATER LIKE A LIVING THING! AND ONLY MR. SPOCK COULD HOPE TO SAVE THIS ALIEN GLOBE THAT HAD THE SPACE PIONEERS TRAPPED UPON IT!

REMAIN CALM, CAPTAIN KIRK! I HAVE MY PLAN NEARLY COMPLETED! WE SHALL CONQUER THIS PLANET'S PROBLEMS!

Captain's Log, Stardate 21:06.7 . . . . DATA REF. . . . 4.00-4.26

CAPTAIN'S LOG, STAR DATE, 21:06.7-- THE ENTERPRISE WAS CRUISING THROUGH GALAXY TELPHA Z...EXPEDITION OPERATIONS WERE NORMAL...UNTIL MR. SPOCK'S RED ALERT BUTTON FLASHED IN MAIN CONTROL...

MR. SPOCK MUST HAVE FOUND SOME ACTION ON HIS PLANET SURVEILLANCE PANEL! LET'S TAKE A LOOK-SEE!

WHAT'S UP, SPOCK? THAT LITTLE PLANET SEEMS TO BE A-OKAY I SEE NOTHING UNUSUAL!

KEEP YOUR EYES ON THOSE NEEDLES! THAT PLANET IS CHANGING ITS CHEMISTRY EVERY FIVE OR TEN MINUTES!

300,000 MILES AWAY, THE PLANET METAMORPHA CONVULSES IN SPACE AS CAPTAIN KIRK, LEADER OF THE ENTERPRISE SPACE PIONEERS, SCOFFS AT MR. SPOCK'S STATEMENT...

OH, COME NOW, SPOCK! CHECK OUT YOUR INSTRUMENTS! THERE HAS TO BE A MALFUNCTION IN THE CONNECTIONS... SUCH THINGS JUST DON'T HAPPEN!

THEY ARE HAPPENING NOW, CAPTAIN KIRK! I'VE DOUBLE CHECKED EVERY PLANETARY SENSORY PICK-UP UNIT! WE'RE IN EXCELLENT WORKING CONDITION!

LET'S MOVE! WE'LL TELEPORT DOWN THERE WITH TWO CREW MEMBERS AND LET SCOTTY HANDLE THE SHIP UPSTAIRS HERE!

DANGEROUS AS IT IS, THE PRESENCE OF THAT 71 METAL MAKES THE RISK WORTH TAKING!

SHORTLY, AS BEAMS ILLUMINATE THE TELEPORTATION CHAMBER...

THE UPHEAVALS ARE EXTENSIVE OVER THE ENTIRE PLANET, CAPTAIN --BUT THERE ARE PLENTY OF EMPTY AREAS WE MIGHT BE SAFE IN!

EXACTLY MY REASONING FOR THE MISSION, MR. SPOCK!

THE RAYS OF LIGHT GROW STRONGER ...GRADUALLY, THE BODIES BEGIN TO DISSOLVE...BLEND INTO THE ETHER OF TIME...

AND A SPLIT SECOND LATER, THE FIGURES MATERIALIZE ON THE PLANET METAMORPHA, THE FANTASTIC, EVER-CHANGING WORLD IN DEEP SPACE...

OUR CALCULATIONS WERE APPARENTLY CORRECT! WE ARE IN A CALM AREA!

BUT SCARCELY ARE THE WORDS OUT OF MR. SPOCK'S MOUTH WHEN...

GR-GREAT GALLOPING GALAXIES-- LOOK!

SPECULATION ON TOUCHDOWN POINT INCORRECT-- WE HAVE BECOME A CRITICAL AREA!

THE SNUB OF A ROCK MASS THRUSTS UPWARD FROM THE EARTH'S CRUST...

WH-WHAT IN BLAZING BLUE COMETS IS *THAT?*

I BELIEVE IT IS A *PEAK,* DR. McCOY... THE TOP OF A...

...MOUNTAIN!

SUDDENLY, THE CATACLYSMIC UPHEAVAL CEASES AND...

LOOK THERE...THE MOUNTAIN'S UPHEAVAL DISLODGED WHAT APPEARS TO BE *MAN-MADE* OBJECTS!

YES, CAPTAIN... APPARENTLY RUINS FROM A LONG-DEAD ALIEN CIVILIZATION!

NO WONDER THEY ARE *LONG DEAD...* TRYING TO EXIST ON THIS UNSTABLE PLANET!

ABRUPTLY, A STRANGE SOUND FILLS THE AIR...

BLOBS OF LIGHT EMERGING FROM THE RUINS!

THE LIGHT FORMS SWIRL TOWARD THE GROUP.. LIKE INTELLIGENCE-DIRECTED THINGS THEY HOME IN ON KIRK AND ONE OF THE CREW...

TH-THEY'RE ATTACKING!

I'LL BLAST THEM WITH MY PHASER!

BUT THE BIZARRE ILLUMINATED FORMS, IMMUNE TO THE PHASER RAY, BOUNCE OFF OF THE PAIR...

THE PHASER SHOTS DIDN'T AFFECT THEM... BUT THEY'RE RETREATING FROM THE CAPTAIN AND CREWMAN JOHNSON! STRANGE...?

ZAP! ZAP!

THE ALIEN BLOBS OF LIGHT REGROUP ... AND AGAIN ATTACK ...

BUT ONCE AGAIN, THE SIX GLOWING FORMS SHY AWAY...

THEY'RE LEAVING McCOY...NOW THEY'RE HEADING FOR SPOCK! WHAT ARE THEY AFTER? WHAT CAN THEY WANT?

LIKE A CLUSTER OF GLOWING, BODYLESS INSECTS, THE FORMS DESCEND UPON MR. SPOCK... ROUND AND ROUND THEY SWIRL...

...BUT I SEEM TO BE FRIGHTENING THEM OFF!

TH-THERE IS NO *BODY* TO THEM...

THEN...

THEY'RE *GONE!*

VANISHED! APPARENTLY DISSIPATED INTO THE ALIEN ATMOSPHERE!

(WHEW!) WELL, THAT'S THAT! NOW LET'S GET ON WITH LOCATING THAT *TI* ORE AND SHOVE OFF BEFORE THIS PLANET DOES ANOTHER FLIP-FLOP!

FOR AN HOUR, THE GROUP COVERS THE TERRAIN WITH DELICATE SPACE-ORE COUNTERS...

COME ON, MR. SPOCK -- GIVE US A HAND! WE WANT TO GET THIS JOB OVER FAST!

I AM MAKING AN ANALYSIS OF THE EARTH CHEMISTRY, CAPTAIN KIRK!

SUDDENLY, AS THE DESPERATE SEARCH FOR THE RARE ORE CONTINUES...

AN-ANOTHER PLANETARY UPHEAVAL! BRACE YOURSELVES, MEN! THERE'S NO TELLING WHAT'S COMING NOW!

THEN, A GEYSER OF WATER SPEWS INTO THE AIR...

WATER! THE ARID AREA IS *TURNING INTO WATER!*

MAKE FOR THE CLIFFSIDE WITH SPOCK! MOVE IT!

BUT THE ONRUSH OF WATER IS TOO RAPID... SWIRLING RAPIDS ENTRAP THE GROUP...

S-SWIM!... FIGHT THE CURRENT... WE'VE *GOT* TO REACH THE LEDGE!

REMAIN CALM, MY FRIENDS! YOU *WILL* BE SAVED!

CAPTAIN KIRK--- CLUTCH THE ROPE! INSTRUCT THE OTHERS TO MAKE A LIFE-CHAIN OF THEIR BODIES BY CLUTCHING YOURS!

G-GOOD THINKING! YOU HEARD HIM, MEN! GRAB HOLD OF ME!

THE LIFE-CHAIN IS FORMED...

HOLD ON TIGHT! I WILL PULL YOU FROM THE WATERS!

GREAT COMETS! WH-WHERE IS SPOCK GETTING THE STRENGTH? H-HE'S PULLING US ALL UP!

FINALLY, ATOP THE LEDGE...

HOW IN THUNDER DID YOU MANAGE IT, MR. SPOCK? -- TOGETHER WE WEIGHED NEARLY EIGHT HUNDRED POUNDS!

EMERGENCY MEASURES OFTEN GIVE ONE EXTRA STRENGTH, CAPTAIN KIRK-- THE ADRENALIN WAS POURING THROUGH MY BODY RAPIDLY!

BUT THERE IS NO TIME FOR IDLE TALK! I HAVE CALCULATED A MEANS TO EXTRACT THE TI ORE...BUT FIRST WE MUST REGULATE THE PLANET--BRING IT BACK TO NORMAL!

BRING IT BACK TO NORMAL?

JUST HOW DO YOU **KNOW** THERE IS A VOLCANIC CRATER BACK THERE?

I KNOW IT IS THERE! DO NOT ASK ME ANY FURTHER QUESTIONS IF YOU WISH TO GET THE TI ORE... **AND SURVIVE!** I WILL JOIN YOU SHORTLY!

PERPLEXED, CAPTAIN KIRK FOLLOWS SPOCK'S DIRECTIONS...

TRANSPORT THE EQUIPMENT DUE SOUTH, MEN!

AS HIS SUPERIOR, I COULD STEP ON SPOCK...BUT PERHAPS HIS VULCAN BACKGROUND HAS **SOMETHING** TO DO WITH THIS...

PERHAPS THIS MAD LITTLE PLANET IS SOMEHOW SIMILAR TO HIS HOME PLANET...IT MAY HAVE SECRETS HE KNOWS ABOUT! I'LL GO ALONG WITH HIM FOR A WHILE!

BUT THE CONFUSED CAPTAIN CAN NOT KNOW THE TERROR THAT IS SEEPING THROUGH MR. SPOCK'S BODY AT THIS VERY MOMENT...

THAT IS **CORRECT,** MR. SPOCK! THE SLING MUST BE **PERFECTLY** PLACED IN THE VOLCANO CRATER...

MMMMMMMM MMMMM

FOR IT IS THE ALIEN LIGHT FORMS THEMSELVES WHO ARE COMMANDING SPOCK'S MIND...

...UNLESS YOUR ATOMIC ROCKET PENETRATES THE MOLTEN CORE OF OUR PLANET PERFECTLY, THE RESULTS WILL BE NIL!

HOW? WHEN DID THIS ALL **HAPPEN** TO YOUR PLANET?

95

THE THOUGHT WAVES OF THE SIX LIGHT FORMS FILL SPOCK'S BRAIN...REVEALING THEIR SECRETS TO HIM...

IT OCCURRED MANY SUN CENTURIES AGO! A GIANT METEORITE PIERCED OUR PLANET IN ITS ONE WEAK AREA...WHERE THE STRUCTURE WAS THIN...

IT WENT THROUGH OUR CRUST, MANTLE, OUTER CORE AND INTO THE MOLTEN MASS OF OUR INNER CORE!

THE MOLECULES OF THE CORE'S MASS WERE CHANGED BY THE CHEMICALS OF THE METEORITE!

"AS THE CHEMICAL REACTION REACHED THE SURFACE THESE TERRIBLE CHANGES BEGAN TO OCCUR...AND OUR BODIES BEGAN TO VAPORIZE..."

OUR PLANET IS DOOMED...TREES SPROUTING UP AMID OUR WATERS WITHIN MINUTES...MOUNTAINS RISING AND FALLING!

AND NOW WE OURSELVES ARE VAPORIZING FROM THE POWER OF THAT ACCURSED METEORITE!

WE NEEDED PHYSICAL FORM TO UNDO THE DAMAGE DONE...AND YOUR VULCAN BODY WAS THE ONLY ONE WE COULD ENTER DUE TO ITS CHEMICAL MAKE-UP!

I UNDERSTAND...!

THE EVOLUTIONARY PROCESSES OF YOUR PLANET WERE SPEEDED UP TRILLIONS OF TIMES OVER! BUT, SHOULD WE CORRECT THE PROBLEM, WILL YOU REVERT TO YOUR *NORMAL* SELVES?

YES!

SPOCK--TALKING TO HIMSELF! WHAT IN THUNDER! WONDER IF HE'S GOT SPACE FATIGUE!

SPOCK!

BUT AS CAPTAIN KIRK SPEAKS, SPOCK HOLDS UP HIS HAND...

SILENCE...PLEASE, CAPTAIN!

THE CHEMICALS YOU NEED FOR THE ROCKET WE MANAGED TO PUT TOGETHER BEFORE WE TOTALLY VANISHED INTO LIGHT FORMS! THEY ARE HIDDEN AT *THIS* LOCATION...

WHAT THE DEVIL IS GOING ON, SPOCK? THIS AIR OF MYSTERY YOU'RE PUTTING ON IS GETTING ON MY NERVES! EVERYTHING IS READY AT THE CRATER!

IT IS ALL RIGHT! I...WAS JUST MAKING A CALCULATION! LET US GO TO THE PENETRATION SITE!

MY ENGINEERING PLANS ARE COMPLETE! I HAVE BUT ONE MORE DETAIL TO COVER!

STAR TREK — THE PERIL OF PLANET QUICK CHANGE

PART II — THE SINISTER GUEST

PREPARING TO BLAST A CHEMICALLY-FILLED ATOMIC ROCKET INTO THE MOLTEN CORE OF THE EVER-CHANGING PLANET METAMORPHA, THE LAUNCHING POINT ON A VOLCANIC CRATER SUDDENLY, CONVULSES, STAGGERING THE ENTERPRISE CREW...

W-WE'VE *HAD* IT, SPOCK! *WHATEVER* YOUR THEORY WAS OF STILLING THIS NIGHTMARISH PLANET IS GONE WITH THE ALIEN WIND...

...I-IF WE GET OUT OF THIS WITH OUR NECKS I'M ORDERING AN *IMMEDIATE* TELEPORTATION BACK TO SHIP!

PLEASE... BE CALM, CAPTAIN KIRK!

THEN... A TELEPATHIC VOICE RESOUNDS IN SPOCK'S BRAIN...

STAND UP AND TELL YOUR PEOPLE TO FOLLOW YOU! *HURRY,* MR. SPOCK!

VERY WELL!

CAPTAIN...MEN! FOLLOW ME! QUICKLY!

AND AS SPOCK LEADS THE CREW AROUND A TURN IN THE CRATER WALL...

WE WILL BE SAFE IN HERE, GENTLEMEN!

WHAT KIND OF A GALAXY GAMBIT HAS SPOCK *GOT?* HE SEEMS TO KNOW THIS PLANET LIKE THE BACK OF HIS VULCAN HAND!

MOMENTS LATER..

THE UPHEAVALS HAVE SUBSIDED! WE CAN CONTINUE *PROJECT PLANET STILL!*

NOW HE'S GOT A CODE NAME FOR THE OPERATION!!

QUICKLY, THE INSCRUTABLE VULCAN MAKES A CALCULATION...

THE DISTURBANCE HAS MOVED THE OPENING OF THE VOLCANIC PIT!! WE MUST REALIGN FOR ROCKET ENTRY!

WITHDRAW THE ROCKET ON ITS LINE... TWO FEET, FOUR INCHES...

ROGER, MR. SPOCK!

SPOCK MOVES TO THE CONTROL PANEL... HIS FINGER REACHES OUT TO PRESS THE BUTTON THAT MEANS LIFE OR DEATH FOR THE PLANET METAMORPHA...

THE ATOMIC ROCKET SLAMS DOWNWARD...THROUGH THE OPENING IN THE VOLCANIC PIT! THEN...DEEP INTO THE PLANET'S HEART THE DIAMOND-TIPPED NOSE OF THE MISSILE DRILLS ITS WAY...

BRRRRR!

DOWN...DOWN IT PLUMMETS INTO THE CONTAMINATED MOLTEN MASS OF THE INNER CORE...

KA-FUIUM!

ALIEN CHEMICALS FROM THE ROCKET ARE HURLED INTO THE FIERY, POLLUTED LIQUID...

THEN, THROUGH THE HOLE BORED BY THE ROCKET AN EERIE, MIST-LIKE MIXTURE ARISES...

UP ABOVE, THE CHEMICAL SPRAY GEYSERS GUSHES OUT...

GREAT RINGS OF SATURN! W-WE'VE HIT SOMETHING DOWN THERE!

WE HAVE SUCCEEDED, CAPTAIN KIRK-- WE HAVE PUNCTURED THE DEADLY HEART OF PLANET METAMORPHA!

LIKE SOME GIGANTIC CLOUD, THE CHEMICAL-FILLED MIST REGENERATES ITSELF AGAIN AND AGAIN... IT MUSHROOMS...

THE WONDER HAS COME TO BE, MR. SPOCK! WITHIN ONE SOLAR DAY OUR MEDICAL MIST WILL HAVE RETURNED OUR WORLD TO NORMAL! WE THANK YOU!

SUDDENLY, THE CREW OF THE ENTERPRISE GAPE AT MR. SPOCK WIDE-EYED...

GR-GREAT GLORY TO BE! TH-THE LIGHT FORMS ... THEY'RE SWIRLING OUT OF MR. SPOCK'S HEAD!

AND THEY'RE MATERIALIZING INTO SOME KIND OF ALIEN, CREATURES!

SPOCK! WHAT'S HAPPENED? WHAT HAVE THEY DONE TO YOU?

AWESTRUCK, THE SPACE PIONEERS WATCH AS SECOND BY SECOND, THE INCREDIBLE OCCURS...

YOUR BRILLIANT VULCAN COLLEAGUE WAS OUR HOST, CAPTAIN KIRK! THROUGH HIS BODY WE WERE ABLE TO SAVE OUR WORLD!

AND NOW WE SHALL MAKE REPAYMENT BY GIVING YOU THE VITAL ORE YOU SEEK! MY NAME IS ZARMAN!

THEN AS THE ALIEN SPEAKS, A FANTASTIC SIGHT CAPTURES THE GROUP...

ZARMAN! LOOK THERE, BEHIND YOU!

AH, YES...

...IT IS OUR TOWN OF *HIDENNA*! AS WE WERE VAPORIZED BY THE POISONED METEORITE, SO IT WAS, TOO! AND NOW AS OUR CHEMICAL ANTIDOTE MIST HAS MATERIALIZED US, HIDENNA ALSO IS RETURNING!

EVEN THE FAMED SPACE PIONEERS ARE DAZED WITH WONDER AT THE REBIRTH OF A TOWN FROM NOTHINGNESS...

THIS WAS MY HOME... AND THE HOME OF MY FRIENDS! ALL OVER OUR PLANET, ONE BY ONE, OTHER TOWNS ARE ALSO RISING!

FANTASTIC, ZARMAN! BUT MR. SPOCK SAID WE HAD AN AGREEMENT IF WE SUCCEEDED IN HELPING YOU!

YES! THE TIANTIANIUM ORE MR. SPOCK'S MIND REVEALED TO US WAS SO VITAL TO YOUR GALAXY! I WILL SHOW YOU THE NEAREST DEPOSIT! COME!

BUT AS ZARMAN LEADS THEM TO A NEARBY AREA...

DIG THERE! BUT PLEASE...EXTRACT BUT TWO HUNDRED GALAXY POUNDS OF THE ORE! WE NEED MUCH OF IT HERE ON METAMORPHA TO KEEP OUR PLANET VITALIZED!

YES...YES! THAT WILL BE SUFFICIENT!

MR. SPOCK! GIVE US A HAND!

NO...I-I CAN NOT, CAPTAIN...I...AM TOO WEAKENED FROM MY ORDEAL!

CERTAINLY! I UNDERSTAND! REST YOURSELF, SPOCK!

MY HEAD...SOMETHING IS NOT CORRECT... MY MIND IS STILL NOT...CLEAR... CONCISE IN THOUGHT!

SUDDENLY, A FRIGHTENING THOUGHT ENLIGHTENS SPOCK'S CLOUDY EYES...

WAIT! SIX LIGHT FORMS ENTERED MY BODY...YES...YES, SIX ENTERED... BUT ONLY FIVE LEFT!

THAT IS TRUE, MR. SPOCK!

I AM STILL WITHIN YOUR BODY...

...YOUR MIND...

...YES, WITHIN YOUR VERY SOUL, MR. SPOCK!

BUT WHY...WHY? WHO ARE YOU? WHY DO YOU BETRAY US SO?

WHILE AT THE ORE SITE...

THAT DOES IT...TWO HUNDRED GALAXY POUNDS! THANK YOU, ZARMAN!

ALL RIGHT, MEN... LET'S GO!

SAY! WHERE IN BLUE THUNDER IS MR. SPOCK?

THERE HE IS, CAPTAIN! HE MUST HAVE BEEN INVESTIGATING THE MATERIALIZED TOWN!

AND AS THEY JOIN THE VULCAN GENIUS, HIS LIPS FRAME WORDS... HIS MIND TRIES TO REVEAL SOMETHING TO CAPTAIN KIRK...

CA-CAPTAIN! THERE IS GREAT DANGER... Y-YOU MUST LISTEN TO ME...!

YES! WHAT IS IT, SPOCK?

BUT THE POWER OF THE SPIRIT FORM WITHIN HIM IS TOO GREAT...

I AM STRONGER THAN YOU, SPOCK! YOU CANNOT REVEAL MY PRESENCE WITHIN YOU! YOU CAN NOT!

CA-CAPTAIN... I...I...A...A POWER...S-SOME-THING WRONG..!

BONES! RADIO SCOTTY TO BEAM US ABOARD FAST... SPOCK'S IN SHOCK! THE REACTION OF THE ALIEN LIGHT CREATURES WITHIN HIM, NO DOUBT!

WE REGRET UPSETTING YOUR FRIEND, CAPTAIN!

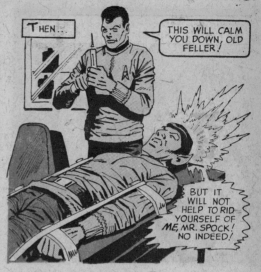

YOU'RE AN ILL MAN, YOU ARE, SIR! BEST YOU LET ME HELP YOU BACK TO SICK BAY!

OOOF!

YOU MUST LET ME GO!

DESPERATELY RESISTING THE FORCE WITHIN HIM, SPOCK STAGGERS LIKE A MAN WITH INVISIVIBLE CHAINS DOWN THE CORRIDOR...

JUST KEEP MYSELF MOVING... MOVING...

SPOCK! YOU ARE HEADING FOR THE TELEPORTATION CHAMBER! WHY? THINK! THINK OF WHAT YOU PLAN SO THAT I CAN KNOW!

WITHIN THE CHAMBER, THE VULCAN LOCKS THE DOOR AND...

WHA..? SPOCK HAS GONE INTO THE TELEPORTATION CHAMBER!

GREAT SATELLITES! HE MUST BE GOING TO TELEPORT HIMSELF BACK TO METAMORPHA!

H-HE'S ACTIVATED THE TELEPORTATION LIGHTS! B-BUT LOOK—HE'S ALSO THROWN OPEN THE RETURN TELEPORTATION SWITCH!

JIM, HE'LL BE SUBJECTED TO OPPOSING FORCES! THEY'LL TEAR HIS MOLECULAR STRUCTURE APART!

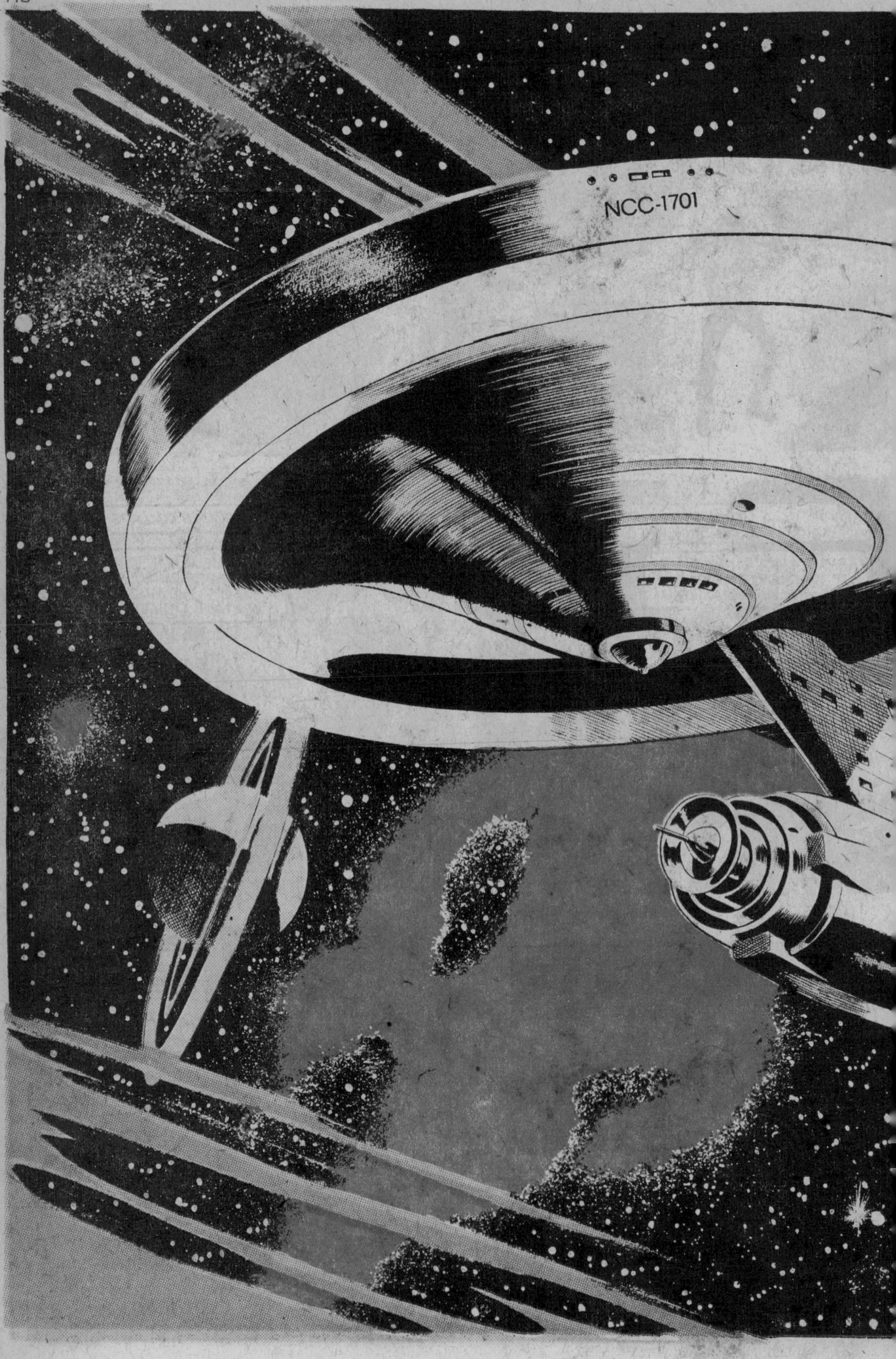
NCC-1701

PORTRAIT OF A STARSHIP:
THE ENTERPRISE

STAR TREK The GHOST PLANET

PART I

HIGH ABOVE THE STRANGE UNPOPULATED WORLD, THE CREW OF THE STAR SHIP ENTERPRISE BATTLE TO SAVE A DOOMED PLANET... BUT THEY CANNOT KNOW OF THE FATE THAT AWAITS THEM ONCE THEY SUCCEED!

OUR MAGNETIC PULL HAS SMASHED THE DEADLY RAINBOW BANDS, CAPTAIN KIRK!

YES, MR. SPOCK! BUT CUT POWER BEFORE THOSE BANDS REACH US OR THEY'LL *PENETRATE THE ENTERPRISE!*

THE VISITORS APPEAR TO HAVE *FREED* OUR PLANET... AND IF SO THEY MUST *DIE!*

10210-909
STAR TREK #5-696

Captain's Log, Stardate 26:06.4 .... DATA REF.... 5.00-5.26

CAPTAIN'S LOG, STAR DATE 26:06.4-- ENTERPRISE MOVING DEEP INTO GALAXY ZELTA... WE HAVE SIGHTED A STRANGE RINGED AREA... IT MAY CONCEAL A PLANET ...INVESTIGATION UNDER WAY...

WHAT DO YOU MAKE OF IT, MR. SPOCK? THEY'RE SIMILAR TO THE RINGS OF SATURN -- BUT NO PLANET IS INDICATED!

I'M CHECKING THEM ON THE SPECTROSCOPE NOW, CAPTAIN KIRK!

THE RINGS ARE COMPOSED OF A COPPER CONTENT, CAPTAIN! THEY ARE CIRCULATING AROUND A... PLANET!

ARE YOU CERTAIN, MR. SPOCK?

AFFIRMATIVE, THE EVIDENCE ON THE SPECTROSCOPE IS UNASSAILABLE!

A PLANET WRAPPED IN RAINBOW RINGS!

ROCKETS ON FULL! SAME COURSE!

NEARING THE SPEED OF LIGHT, THE QUEEN SHIP OF THE STAR FLEET PLUMMETS TOWARD THE UNKNOWN PLANET...

THE COPPER CONTENT...IS IT DANGEROUS TO US?

NO! THERE IS A MINOR MAGNETIC FIELD BUT WE HAVE THE THRUST TO OVERCOME IT!

HOWEVER, THERE WILL BE TURBULENCE!

SECURE SEAT BELTS!

LIKE A GIANT, FIRE-BREATHING ANIMAL THE ENTERPRISE WHIPLASHES INTO THE MULTICOLORED MAGNETIC FIELD RINGS...

STABILIZERS! RIG THE STABILIZERS FOR EXTREME PRESSURE! MR. SPOCK! WHAT IS THE DEPTH WE MUST PENETRATE?

TWO LUNAR MILES! OBSERVE! THERE TO STARBOARD... A SECTION OF PLANET IS COMING INTO VIEW!

THEN, THE TURBULENCE CEASES... AND THE SPACE CRAFT CAREENS FREE ABOVE A MAJESTIC NEW WORLD...

GR-GREAT NOVAS! YOU WERE CORRECT, MR. SPOCK -- A BRAND NEW PLANET LOCKED BEHIND THOSE RAINBOW RINGS!

AND A MOST UNUSUAL ONE, CAPTAIN! I'M GETTING RADIOACTIVE IMPULSES!

RADIOACTIVITY! CAN YOU PINPOINT IT?

NO, IT IS VERY FAINT! BUT IT IS PRESENT!

TRIGGER TELESCOPIC VIEW CAMERA!

AN EMPTY CITY ...NOT A CITIZEN, VEHICLE OR MOVING THING! WHAT DO YOU MAKE OF IT, MR. SPOCK?

ONE CANNOT JUDGE SO QUICKLY! PERHAPS A GHOST TOWN!!

SHALL WE RECONNOITER THE AREA FOR A FEW HOURS, CAPTAIN?

NO...

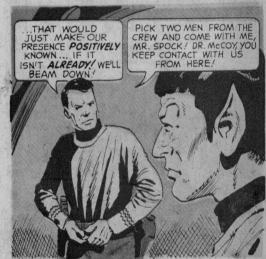

..THAT WOULD JUST MAKE OUR PRESENCE POSITIVELY KNOWN ... IF IT ISN'T ALREADY! WE'LL BEAM DOWN!

PICK TWO MEN FROM THE CREW AND COME WITH ME, MR. SPOCK! DR. McCOY, YOU KEEP CONTACT WITH US FROM HERE!

MOMENTS LATER, BEAMS IN THE TRANSPORT CHAMBER ILLUMINATE THE EXPLORATION TEAM ...

AND A MICRO-SECOND LATER, THE FOUR-MAN TEAM MATERIALIZES ON THE MYSTERIOUS *GHOST PLANET*...

SUDDENLY, A HOLLOW VOICE BOOMS OUT IN THE EMPTY SQUARE...

WELCOME, VISITORS! TRANSPORTATION IS ENROUTE FOR YOU!

WHAT DO YOU MAKE OF IT, MR. SPOCK? SOME TYPE OF MECHANIZED CIVILIZATION?

NEGATIVE, CAPTAIN! IF YOU NOTICE, THE AREA DOES NOT APPEAR *LIVED* IN!

...AND LOOK OVER *THERE!*

PART OF THE CITY IN *RUINS!* A HOLOCAUST! PERHAPS A CITY BURNED OUT!

I BELIEVE *NOT!* THERE ARE DEEP INDENTATIONS IN THE GROUND...

...SIMILAR TO THOSE MADE BY BOMBING DURING A *WAR!*

HERE'S OUR VEHICLE ROBOT CONTROLLED! KEEP YOUR PHASERS READIED, PEOPLE!

THIS IS EERIE, CAPTAIN! SHOULD WE GO THROUGH WITH IT?

WE'RE PREPARED! PEOPLE WITH A CIVILIZATION LIKE THIS CAN'T BE FOOLS--THEY MUST KNOW WE HAVE A SHIP HOVERING ABOVE THAT COULD DESTROY THEM AT ANY SIGN OF TREACHERY!

SHORTLY, THE VEHICLE SLOWS AND...

A ROBOT-- MOTIONING US INSIDE!

THIS APPEARS TO BE THEIR CENTRAL COMMUNICATIONS BUILDING! CAPTAIN, OBSERVE THE MANY ANTENNAE...

PLEASE... TAKE YOUR... SEATS!

VERY DRAMATIC! AT LEAST THEY SPEAK THE INTERPLANETARY LANGUAGE ESPERANTA!

WE KNOW... YOU ARE... CONFUSED... IT WILL BE EXPLAINED... BUT YOU MUST... BELIEVE WE ARE FRIENDLY ...NOW THE GOVERNMENT HEADS WILL ADDRESS YOU!

ABRUPTLY, THE GIANT SCREEN GLISTENS... TWO MAMMOTH HEADS APPEAR...

PLEASE LET US INTRODUCE OURSELVES! WE ARE THE TWIN SUPREMES OF PLANET NUMERO UNO! I AM JUSTIN!

AND I AM JUSTIN! WE RULE TOGETHER!

AND *I* AM *CAPTAIN KIRK* OF THE *STAR SHIP ENTERPRISE!* OUR MISSION IS TO AID THOSE OF THE PLANETARY SYSTEM WHO MAY BE IN NEED!

BUT THE TREATMENT YOU OFFER IS INSULTING! EITHER IDENTIFY YOURSELVES PROPERLY OR WE WILL *LEAVE!*

PLEASE... I APOLOGIZE... *WE* APOLOGIZE! CAPTAIN KIRK--IF YOU WILL BE PATIENT AND HEAR OUR TERRIBLE STORY YOU WILL UNDERSTAND!

VERY WELL! *SPEAK!*

AND AS JUSTIN ONE SPEAKS, THE SCREEN ENLARGES...TO TAKE IN A TERRIFYING SIGHT...

IT WAS JUST A LUNAR SUN AGO THAT THE TERROR MOVED IN UPON OUR PLANET...THE TERRIBLE RAINBOW RINGS THAT WERE SOON TO THROTTLE AND DRIVE US FROM THE PLANET OF OUR ANCESTORS...

THE VERY SIGHT OF THE RINGS STRUCK TERROR INTO THE HEARTS OF MY PEOPLE...

AND AS THE DAYS PASSED, THE MENACE OF THE EERIE RINGS WAS TO BE KNOWN TO US ALL... *PHYSICALLY!*

FOR THE OMINOUS BANDS EMITTED A STRANGE COPPER RADIATION THAT AFFECTED OUR BODIES!

NO SUBSTANCE KNOWN CAN STOP THE RADIATION, JUSTIN 1! OUR ENTIRE POPULATION WILL PERISH!

BUT WE CANNOT STAND BY AND ALLOW OUR RACE TO BECOME EXTINCT! *SOMETHING* MUST BE DONE!

THE BUILDING OF TWO ARTIFICIAL SATELLITES WENT UNDER EMERGENCY CONSTRUCTION...

AND WITHIN A MONTH'S TIME, THE UNOITE EXODUS TO THE SATELLITES WAS UNDERWAY! IT WAS EXTREMELY SUCCESSFUL...

ENOUGH! AND NOW LET'S GIVE THESE ROBOTS A *HOT-FOOT!*

I GET IT--THE WATER WILL ACT AS A CONDUCTOR FOR THE HIGH FREQUENCY BATTERY CHARGES OF OUR TRANSISTORS! BUT WILL THE CHARGE BE *STRONG* ENOUGH?

AT LEAST IT'S GIVING THEM A GOOD JOLT...

CONGRATULATIONS, MR. SPOCK--YOU MADE JUNK HEAPS OUT OF THEM!

AND NOW LET US LEARN WHAT IS BEHIND THAT DOOR-- IMPORTANT ENOUGH TO PROGRAM HOSTILITY INTO THOSE ROBOT GUARDS!

WHY...THIS MUST BE THE UNOITE *WAR ROOM!* BUT WHY WOULD A PEACEFUL RACE NEED SUCH A ROOM?

PERHAPS THE ANSWER CAN BE FOUND WITHIN THOSE TOP SECRET FILES, CAPTAIN!

THE CURIOUS HUMANS RUMMAGE THROUGH THE FILES--AND SUDDENLY FREEZE IN THEIR TRACKS AS...

HERE IS THE ANSWER TO OUR QUESTION, CAPTAIN--*OBSERVE THESE PHOTOGRAPHS!*

NO WONDER THEY PROGRAMMED THEIR ROBOTS TO GUARD THIS ROOM WITH THEIR MECHANICAL "LIVES"!

THE PLANET NUMERO UNO WAS ENGAGED IN A *DEADLY WAR!* THESE ARE NOT THE HELPLESS PEACE-LOVING PEOPLE THEY FEIGN TO BE!

THAT WOULD SEEM LOGICAL!

IT FOLLOWS THAT THEY WERE *FORCED* TO CALL A TRUCE WHEN THE DEADLY RINGS ENCIRCLED THE PLANET!

YES...

...AND ONCE WE HAVE *FREED* THEM OF THE YOKE OF PEACE, THEY WILL *CONTINUE* THE FIGHT! WE'LL HAVE TO SHAKE THEM UP A BIT!

AND AS THE *TWIN SUPREMES* APPEAR ON THE SCREEN AGAIN...

WHAT NEWS? CAN YOU HELP US?

ER... VERY WELL, CAPTAIN!

MEET US ABOARD OUR SHIP IN ONE HOUR! THIS IS *URGENT! BE* THERE!

AN HOUR LATER, THE CAPTAIN AND HIS MEN ARE BACK ABOARD THE ENTERPRISE...

THIS IS IT... A *SUMMIT MEETING IN SPACE!*

STAR TREK The GHOST PLANET
PART II

As TWIN SUPREMES OF THE PLANET NUMERO UNO ENTER THE ENTERPRISE, KIRK CONFRONTS THEM WITH THE PHOTOGRAPHIC EVIDENCE THAT THEY WERE AT WAR AND...

CEASE! I-I WILL NOT RESIST FURTHER!

INDEED, THEY ARE INSTINCTIVELY BRACED TO DO BATTLE! THE MOMENT YOU SHOWED THEM THE PHOTOGRAPHS THEIR HANDS FLEW TO THEIR WEAPONS, CAPTAIN KIRK!

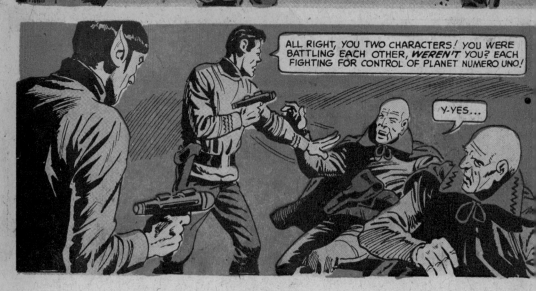

ALL RIGHT, YOU TWO CHARACTERS! YOU WERE BATTLING EACH OTHER, WEREN'T YOU? EACH FIGHTING FOR CONTROL OF PLANET NUMERO UNO!

Y-YES...

AND THEN THE DOOM RINGS CAME AND YOU HAD TO STOP THE WAR TO SAVE *BOTH* YOUR NECKS?

WE... CAN NOT DENY THE FACTS!

HERE'S ANOTHER FACT! OUR JOB IS TO BRING *PEACE* TO THE GALAXIES! WE BELIEVE IT BEST TO LET YOUR CIVILIZATION *DIE OUT!*

NO... NO!

WHY *NOT?* IF WE MAKE IT POSSIBLE FOR YOU TO RETURN FROM THE SATELLITES YOU'LL JUST SLAUGHTER YOURSELVES ANYWAY!

BUT WE CANNOT *DO* THAT! THERE ARE *NO* WEAPONS LEFT!

WHAT FOOLS DO YOU THINK WE ARE? YOU'LL MAKE MORE WAR! NO... YOU REMAIN ON YOUR DYING SATELLITES!

WAIT! I HAVE A PLAN...

...LEAVE VISUAL *DETECTORS* OVER OUR MANUFACTURING AREAS! FROM SPACE YOU CAN *OBSERVE* US FOR YEARS! IF WE START TO BUILD AGAIN YOU CAN DESTROY US BY TIME DEVICES LEFT BEHIND!

WELL, SPOCK...

IT IS CONSTRUCTIVELY PUT! OUR WORK IS TO HELP PLANETS— NOT WATCH THEM DIE!

VERY WELL! RETURN TO YOUR SATELLITES AT ONCE! THE ENTERPRISE HAS WORK TO DO! YOU WILL BE INFORMED!

SPOCK..!

WITHIN THE LAB ROOM OF THE STAR SHIP ENTERPRISE KIRK AND SPOCK STUDY THE PROBLEM...

IF THE FULL FORCE OF OUR MAGNETIC GENERATORS CAN MAKE A CRACK IN ONE SECTION OF THE RINGS, BEND IT SHARPLY ENOUGH...

..WE MAY BE ABLE TO PULL ALL THE DOOM RINGS THROUGH IT INTO SPACE!

RIGHT, MR. SPOCK! THAT'S OUR ONLY SHOT! LET'S GO!

FIVE MINUTES LATER, THE FULL FORCE OF THE ENTERPRISE'S MAGNETIC GENERATORS ARE PROPELLED DOWNWARD...

129

A SECTION OF THE COPPER-FILLED RINGS BEND AS THE RAYS HIT...

BUT NOT STRONG *ENOUGH!* KEEP TRYING!

WE'RE GETTING A STRONG POSITIVE REACTION, CAPTAIN!

MINUTE AFTER MINUTE, THE POWERFUL MAGNETIC FORCE DRAWS UPON THE RINGS...

WE'VE FAILED! OUR MAGNETIC GENERATORS ARE BEING WEAKENED... FURTHER ATTEMPT IS USELESS!

PERHAPS THERE IS *ANOTHER* MEANS, CAPTAIN!

IF WE DREW THE POWER OF THE SATELLITES' MAGNETIC FIELD INTO OUR GENERATORS, THE ADDED POWER MIGHT...

YOU'VE HIT IT, MR. SPOCK! COMMENCE OPERATION!

QUICKLY, ELECTRONIC "RIFLES" ARE AIMED AT THE MAGNETIC FIELD OF THE TWIN SATELLITES...

IT'S WORKING, MR. SPOCK! WE'RE SUCKING IN THE MAGNETIC FIELDS!

WE'VE GOT THEM ALL...EVERY DEADLY RING! PREPARE TO CUT POWERS!

OF COURSE! OTHERWISE THEY WOULD COLLIDE WITH THE ENTERPRISE...ENTER OUR SHIP ITSELF!

AT THE PRECISE MOMENT, MR. SPOCK CUTS OFF THE POWER...

NOW! WE HAVE THEM GOING FAST ENOUGH TO CONTINUE, I BELIEVE, CAPTAIN!

OUT INTO DEEP SPACE THE NOW CONVULSING BEAMS STREAK...

..WHERE SOME MYSTERIOUS SOLAR ACTION BURSTS THEM ASUNDER...

WHILE WITHIN THE ENTERPRISE, JOYOUS WORD IS RECEIVED FROM THE TWIN SUPREMES...

WONDERFUL WORK, FRIENDS! WE SHALL RETURN TO OUR HOME AT ONCE!

NO, WAIT...

THERE MAY HAVE BEEN A DANGEROUS COPPER CONTENT DISCHARGED DOWN FROM THE REACTION! WE'LL TEST THE AREA FIRST!

I SHALL BRING THE TEST GEAR TO THE TRANSPORTING CHAMBER!

SOON AFTER...

IF THERE ARE SIGNS OF COPPER PENETRATION IT MAY BE YEARS BEFORE THEY CAN RETURN, MR. SPOCK!

WE SHALL SOON KNOW, CAPTAIN! THIS AREA HERE WAS MOST VULNERABLE!

SUDDENLY, A GEIGER COUNTER CLICKS...

COPPER RADIATION, MR. SPOCK?

NO, CAPTAIN!

CLICK CLICK CLICK CLICK CLICK CLICK

...ATOMIC RADIATION, SIR--COMING FROM THAT AREA!

THE VISITOR SEEKS TO BLUFF US, JUSTIN II!

IT WILL NOT SAVE HIS LIFE, JUSTIN I!

WHAT I SAY CAN MOST CERTAINLY SAVE *YOURS*...

...OBSERVE FOR YOURSELVES... THERE IN THE HEAVENS ABOVE YOUR PLANET!

ABRUPTLY, THE PAIR GAPE IN AWE AS THEY LOOK SPACEWARD...

T-THE RAINBOW BANDS W-WITH COPPER DEATH... THEY HAVE *RETURNED!*

B-BUT HOW IS IT *POSSIBLE?* WE *SAW* THEM *DESTROYED* IN DEEP SPACE!

WH-WHAT IN THUNDER?

WHILE DESTROYING THE BANDS WE SOLVED THEIR SECRET! AT A MOMENT'S NOTICE WE CAN ENCIRCLE YOUR PLANET AGAIN WITH THEM!

NOW! EITHER DROP YOUR GUNS OR FIRE! IF *WE* DIE YOUR ENTIRE CIVILIZATION PERISHES!

NO...NO! YOU MAY GO FREE! JUST TAKE YOUR DEADLY BANDS WITH YOU!

Captain's Log, Stardate 23:00.9 . . . . DATA REF. . . . 6.00-6.32

CAPTAIN'S LOG, STAR DATE, 23:009-- TOP BRASS STUDIED A CURIOUS PICK-UP ON THE SCREEN OF THE ENTERPRISE'S TV SPACE SCANNER...

THE OPERATORS HAVE BEEN TRACKING THOSE U.B.* BLIPS SINCE THEY APPEARED IN THE ALPHO GALAXY! WHAT DO YOU MAKE OF THEM, MR. SPOCK?

HMM·M...ALTHOUGH THEY ARE ON A DIRECT COURSE WITH ONE ANOTHER THERE'S STILL A BILLION-MILE RANGE BETWEEN THEM...

* U.B.--UNIDENTIFIED BODY

...AND THE ODDS AGAINST COLLISION ARE JUST ABOUT THAT GREAT! STILL, CAPTAIN, WE'D BETTER KEEP OUR SPACE EYES ON THEM!

I AGREE! AND SINCE WE'RE THE CLOSEST SHIP TO THEM IN THE STAR FLEET, I'M GO-ING TO SET CRUISE COURSE IN THAT DIRECTION!

FIVE DAYS LATER A STARTLING ANNOUNCEMENT COMES OVER THE LOUDSPEAKER...

COMMUNICATIONS HERE, SIR! THOSE BLIPS ON OUR TV SCANNER--WE'VE IDENTIFIED THEM! THEY'RE... PLANETS!

PLANETS...IN THE GALAXY AND ORBITING ALPHO! QUITE INCON-CEIVABLE--THIS MUST BE CHECKED OUT IMMEDIATELY, CAPTAIN!

THERE ARE OUR SPACE BOGIES--AND STILL ON COLLISION COURSE! MR. SPOCK...WHAT IF THEY SHOULD HIT...?

AT THEIR ESTIMATED POINT OF CONTACT, THE RESULTS WOULD BE CATASTROPHIC, SCOTTY!

THE SHOCK WAVES UPON IMPACT ALONE WOULD PITCH MANY OF THE ALPHO PLANETS OUT OF ORBIT...TO BURN IN SPACE!

WE STILL DON'T KNOW IF THOSE FOREIGN PLANETS ARE INHABITED-- TRY TO RAISE THEM ON OUR SOS SPACE FREQUENCY, OPERATOR...

AYE, SIR!

NERVES DRAW TAUT AS THE FRANTIC SIGNAL IS SENT FROM THE SPACECRAFT TIME AND AGAIN! BUT...

NEGATIVE, CAPTAIN!

GOOD! NOW OUR ACTION IS CLEAR-- DESTROY ONE OF THE PLANETS AND ELIMINATE THE COLLISION THREAT!

THERE IS STILL AMPLE TIME TO INTERCEPT EITHER PLANET WELL BEFORE ESTIMATED COLLISION TIME, CAPTAIN...

WE'RE CLOSEST BY SEVERAL THOUSAND GALAXY MILES TO F.P.-1*

GIVE THE NAVIGATOR THAT COURSE, MR. SPOCK!

* FOREIGN PLANET-1

THE CRUISING PACE OF THE ENTERPRISE IS ABRUPTLY BROKEN BY A SINGLE COMMAND AND...

UNDER FULL ROCKET THRUST, CAPTAIN!

LIKE A MISSILE HOMING ON TARGET, THE SPACE-CRAFT REACHES ITS OBJECTIVE A GALAXY-DAY LATER...

NO SIGN OF LIFE-- NOT SO MUCH AS A SHRUB! NO WONDER WE DIDN'T RECEIVE A REPLY FROM OUR SOS TRANSMISSION, CAPTAIN!

WE'LL LAND A TEAM TO PLANT THE HYDROGEN CHARGES AT ONCE! I'LL LEAD THE GROUP... MR. SPOCK AND SCOTTY WILL ACCOMPANY ME!

THE CREW IN THE TRANSPORTER ROOM IS ON THE ALERT! BEAMS ILLUMINATE THE LANDING PARTY UNTIL THEIR BODIES GRADUALLY DISSOLVE...

AND BLEND INTO THE ETHER OF TIME AND SPACE UNTIL MATERIALIZATION OCCURS ON THE PLANET BELOW...

ATMOSPHERE FAVORABLE... NO NEED FOR FILTER MASKS...

CAPTAIN! THOSE GROWTHS ATOP THE DOMES... THEY'RE *MOVING!*

SPLASH!

WE'VE BEEN ATTACKED! THE PLANET *IS* INHABITED!

A WARMING GLOW OF BRILLIANT LIGHT FILLS THE CHAMBER AND...

WHAT'S HAPPENING? IS THIS ANOTHER TRICK? IF IT *IS*...

NO, NO! THAT IS OUR *SUN*, GENTLEMEN FROM THE ENTERPRISE!

IT IS AN *ARTIFICIAL* SUN... MADE MANY CENTURIES AGO WHEN OUR OWN SUN DIED AND LEFT US A COLD AND DYING WORLD!

BUT, OF COURSE, YOU COULD NOT UNDERSTAND! COME... LET ME SHOW YOU HOW WE SURVIVE HERE ON *THE PLANET MORTI!*

IT HAS TAKEN US MANY TIME-SPACE CENTURIES TO DEVELOP...

THINK WE'RE BEING BOONDOGGLED..."PUT ON," MR. SPOCK?

I... DO NOT *THINK* SO, CAPTAIN!

THEN...

Y!!!IPES! BE-BEJABBERS! LOOK AT *THAT!*

IN AWE, THE TRIO LOOKS DOWN FIVE HUNDRED FEET UPON A WORLD WITHIN A WORLD...

A RURAL FARM LAND... RIVERS, CATTLE!

INDEED THERE *ARE*, CAPTAIN KIRK! QUITE OBVIOUSLY THIS MASSIVE FARMLAND AND OTHERS SUPPLY THE FOOD FOR PLANET MORTI!

A *DOZEN* OTHERS, STRANGER!

OUR AGRICULTURAL LANDS STRETCH FOR A HUNDRED MILES BENEATH THE SURFACE, FLOURISHING FROM AS MANY DOMES WHICH ADMIT THE LIFE-GIVING RAYS FROM OUR ARTIFICIAL SUN!

148

THEN, EVER SINCE YOUR PLANET BEGAN TO DIE YOUR PEOPLE HAVE LIVED ON THE SURFACE AND FARMED FOR YOUR FOOD BELOW!

THAT IS CORRECT! WE HAVE NO BUSINESS, NO GREAT INDUSTRIES... WE MERELY SURVIVE!

ONE THING, SIR! I CAN NOT UNDERSTAND WHY WE COULD NOT OBSERVE YOUR ARTIFICIAL SUN VIA OUR OBSERVATIONS OF YOUR PLANET!

AH, THAT IS QUITE SIMPLE...

TO CONSERVE ITS VITAL THERMO-HYDROGEN FUEL WE TRIGGER THE SUN FORCE BUT *FIVE HOURS* A DAY! THAT IS QUITE SUFFICIENT!

CERTAINLY! AND THE ROTATION OF YOUR PLANET KEPT THE SUN SIDE AWAY FROM US DURING OUR JOURNEY HERE! QUITE ASTONISHING!

TIME'S RUNNING OUT, MR. SPOCK!

YES! WITH EACH HOUR THE PLANETS' SPEED TOWARD EACH OTHER ACCELERATES 8,108 GALAXY MILES! WE MUST LEAVE FOR F.P.-2 IMMEDIATELY!

MOMENTS LATER, AS THE TRANSPORTING MACHINE FROM THE ENTERPRISE BEGINS TO BLEND THE THREE INTO THE ETHER OF TIME...

WE WILL KEEP YOU INFORMED! HAVE COURAGE, MY FRIEND!

THANK YOU, SPACE PIONEERS! IT IS GOOD TO KNOW WE HAVE NEW FRIENDS IN THIS GALAXY!

AND ONCE ABOARD THE ENTERPRISE...

ROCKET CONTROL! FULL ROCKETS THRUST TOWARD FOREIGN PLANET TWO!

AYE, AYE, SIR!

ALL YOUR SPECTROSCOPE READINGS INDICATE *NO LIFE*, MR. SPOCK!

AFFIRMATIVE!

ON THE BASIS OF OXYGEN AND SURFACE FOLIAGE! LIFE AS WE *KNOW* IT, THAT IS!

AND HOURS LATER, AS THE ENTERPRISE NUDGES THE SPEED OF LIGHT IN HER DESPERATE FLIGHT TOWARD THE DOOMED PLANET...

ORE CONTENT OF PLANET GETTING STRONGER! IT IS OF *UNKNOWN* MATTER!

READY RETRO ROCKETS! PREPARE FOR ORBITING THRUST!

HIGH *ORE* CONTENT, I SHOULD *THINK* SO! THERE APPEARS TO BE NOTHING DOWN THERE BUT IRON MOUNTAINS!

MOUNTAINS... BUT NOT *IRON*, CAPTAIN!

THE STAR SHIP ENTERPRISE ORBITS FOREIGN PLANET TWO, SEEKING SIGNS OF LIFE...

NO, CAPTAIN, THOSE MOUNTAINS ARE NOT COMPOSED OF *IRON!* THE SPECTROSCOPE READINGS INDICATE AN UNKNOWN, HIGHLY ACTIVE METAL CONTENT!

RATHER STRANGE, EH, MR. SPOCK!

THEN, AS THE CRAFT DIVES FOR CLOSER SURVEYING...

YI-YIKES!

SCOTTY! SU-SUFFERING HANNAH--HE'S BEEN *SLAMMED* INTO THE CHAMBER WALL!

SOME POWER... *PULLING* HIM!

WHAT IS IT YOU HAVE IN YOUR POCKET? SOME IMMENSELY POWERFUL FORCE IS REACTING UPON IT!

I...I...

...PICKED UP A PIECE OF ROCK FROM F.P.-1 WHEN WE LANDED... AS A-A SOUVENIR...

IT IS BEING *MAGNETIZED* FROM BELOW...

151

THEN, AS THE ORE IS RIPPED FROM MR. SPOCK'S HANDS...

I CAN NOT HOLD IT! *RIGHT THE SHIP! HURRY!!*

CRASH!

LEVEL OFF!

A FANTASTIC FORCE...EMANATING FROM THE TERRAIN OF F.P.-2 AND DRAWING UPON THAT PIECE OF ROCK...STRONGER THAN THE MOST POWERFUL ELECTRO MAGNET!

BUT *HOW?* WHY?

AND AS THE SPACE CRAFT LEVELS OFF, IT CREATES A BIZARRE EFFECT ON SCOTTY'S PIECE OF ORE...

OBSERVE, AS THE SHIP LEVELS...

...THE MAGNETIC PULL IS CHANGING DIRECTION...

...PULLING THE ROCK DOWNWARD TOWARD THE PLANET!

THERE IS THE ANSWER TO OUR *PLANET COLLISION* PROBLEM, CAPTAIN!! THE ORE IN THOSE MOUNTAIN RANGES IS REACTING UPON THE CRUST OF F.P.-1...

...THE MAGNETIC INFLUENCE IS SO POWERFUL IT SURGES THROUGH SPACE AND IS DRAWING THE PLANET TOWARD IT! A FREAK GALAXY CHEMISTRY IS CREATING THIS DISASTER!

THEN THE SOLUTION IS *SIMPLE*, MR. SPOCK--ATOMIZE THE MOUNTAINS OUT OF EXISTENCE AND ELIMINATE THE PROBLEM!

ASSUMING THERE IS NO LIFE THERE!

THERE CAN'T BE! WE'VE ORBITED THE PLANET THREE TIMES... NOT A SPARK OF LIFE SEEN! NO SURFACE DOMES... NOTHING!

WAIT!

BEFORE WE TRANSPORT DOWN LET US USE THAT ORE AS A TEST PIECE! WE MAY BE ABLE TO FIND A MINERAL THAT WILL *BREAK* THE MAGNETIC PULL!

GOOD!

MOMENTS LATER, FOUR STRONG MEN ARE NEEDED TO WITHSTAND THE FANTASTIC PULL OF THE MOUNTAIN METAL AGAINST F.P.-1'S ORE...

REALIGN THE LAB VISE FOR OVERHEAD EXPERIMENT!

RIGHT, MR. SPOCK!

THEN...

IF WE CAN FIND A METAL WITH THE RIGHT CHEMICAL CONTENT TO *BREAK* THE PULL BETWEEN F.P.-2'S MOUNTAIN METAL AND F.P.-1'S ORE WE CAN BUILD A *SPACE-BREAK* BETWEEN THEM!

YES, IT WOULD GIVE US TIME TO DESTROY THE MOUNTAINS!

FOR TWO HOURS MR. SPOCK LABORS TO CRACK THE SECRET, BUT...

NO LUCK... I HAVE GONE THROUGH 101 METALS IN OUR CHEMICAL TABLE BUT THE MAGNETIC FORCE IS THE *SAME!*

THAT DOES IT!

THE TRANSPORTER ROOM, DR. McCOY, MR. SPOCK... SCOTTY! WE CAN'T WASTE ANOTHER MINUTE!

AS THE FOUR TAKE THEIR PLACES IN THE TRANSPORTER ROOM, BEAMS FROM ABOVE ILLUMINATE THEM...

IT MAY TAKE A LONG TIME TO DEMOLISH THOSE MAGNETIC MOUNTAINS! AND COLLISION TIME IS *SHORT!*

INSTANTS LATER, THE MEN ARE TRANSPORTED THROUGH SPACE TO APPEAR ON THE BIZARRE CELESTIAL BODY KNOWN AS FOREIGN PLANET TWO...

MATERIALIZATION COMPLETE! TRANSPORT ATOMIC EXPLOSIVE CHARGES DOWN AT ONCE!

AYE, AYE CAPTAIN!

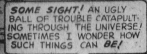

SOME SIGHT! AN UGLY BALL OF TROUBLE CATAPULTING THROUGH THE UNIVERSE! SOMETIMES I WONDER HOW SUCH THINGS CAN BE!

WE HAVE MUCH TO LEARN IN THE FAR REACHES OF SPACE YET, CAPTAIN!

FROM THE APPEARANCE OF THE TERRAIN I CALCULATE ABOUT TWO TONS OF MINI-ATOMIC CHARGES WILL BE REQUIRED TO MELT THE MOUNTAIN RANGE!

OUR EXPLOSIVES!

IF THERE WAS TIME I'D BLOW THE WHOLE CUSSED PLANET UP... IT'S CERTAINLY NO USE TO THE GALAXY!

NO, I GATHER NOT, CAPTAIN, UNLESS, OF COURSE...

IT HAS SOME UNKNOWN PURPOSE AMONG THE STARS ... SUCH AS EARTH MUST HAVE HAD AT ONE TIME!

OH, COME ON... SPARE ME THAT VULCAN PHILOSOPHY OF YOURS RIGHT NOW, MR. SPOCK!

DR. McCOY, YOU AND SCOTTY TAKE THAT END OF THE RANGE! MR. SPOCK AND I WILL COVER THIS! USE YOUR PHASERS CAREFULLY MAKING THE DETONATION HOLES!

FOR FOUR TENSE HOURS THE SPACE PIONEERS PREPARE FOR *OPERATION MOUNTAIN BLAST!* THEIR PHASERS TUNNEL HOLES DEEP INSIDE THE METALLIC RANGE FOR CHARGES TO BE PLACED...

BZzzzzz

BZzzzz

FINALLY, ALL IS *"GO"...*

ALL CHARGES SET, CAPTAIN!

WE'RE READY TO ROLL HERE ALSO! RENDEZVOUS AT THE TRANSPORTER SITE... *ON THE DOUBLE!*

AND AS THE TEAM PREPARES TO VANISH INTO THE ETHER OF TIME FOR RETURN TO THE SHIP...

WELL, THAT IS *THAT,* CAPTAIN! WE MUST *BE WELL* OUT OF RANGE BEFORE DETONATION... POWERFUL CHARGES INDEED!

YES! READY TO THROW THE TRANSPORTER SWITCH!

SUDDENLY...

??

WAIT!

WHAT *IS* IT, SPOCK? WHAT'S *WRONG?*

I THOUGHT I SAW SOMETHING *MOVE...* A *LIVING FORM!*

INTO THE DEPTHS OF THE MOUNTAIN SPOCK TUMBLES...

DOWN...DOWN TOWARD A YAWNING CAVERN FAR BELOW HIS BODY HURTLES...

WHILE ABOVE...

A TUNNEL... INTO THE MOUNTAIN!

SPOCK *DID* SEE SOMETHING...AND THEY'VE *GOT* HIM! BREAK OUT YOUR FLARE LIGHTS! *HURRY!*

AN *ALIEN*-- THE ONE WHO TRAPPED MR. SPOCK, NO DOUBT! *LET'S GO!*

BELOW SPOCK BURSTS INTO A GLARE OF WHITE LIGHT...

GR-GREAT *ZOUNDS!*

A SHOCKING PANORAMA OF A CIVILIZATION BENEATH THE MOUNTAINS UNFOLDS BEFORE SPOCK'S STARTLED EYES...

A WORLD... AN *INTELLIGENT PEOPLE* ...LIVING *BENEATH* THE EARTH'S CRUST!

WHO ARE YOU, ALIEN INTRUDER? WHY DO YOU SEEK ENTRANCE INTO OUR LAND?

AND AS THE ALIEN SENTRY PLUMMETS INTO THE CHAMBER...

MORE ENEMIES COMING!

WAIT! WE ARE NOT FOES!

WE HAVE COME TO *WARN* YOU OF AN APPROACHING DISASTER TO YOUR PLANET AND TRY TO *SAVE* YOUR CIVILIZATION!

SO! BRING THEM TO MY THRONE CHAMBER...

FOOOSH!

FOOOSH!

...BUT *LIGHT-BIND* THEM WHILE I WEIGH THE *TRUTH* OF THEIR WORDS!

IN THE MAGNIFICENT SPLENDOR OF THE UNDERGROUND WORLD THE STRANGE LEADER EYES HIS CAPTIVES KEENLY...

YOU CAME TO *WARN* US? HOW DID YOU *KNOW* OF US *INICRUST* PEOPLES? NO OTHERS IN THE GALAXY REALIZE WE *EXIST!*

WE DID NOT KNOW OF YOU!

IT WAS YOUR *METALLIC* MOUNTAINS THAT DREW US HERE! THE MINERALS IN THEM ARE DRAWING YOUR PLANET TO A COLLISION COURSE WITH ANOTHER!

CONTINUE!

AND WHEN SPOCK HAS EXPLAINED THE IMPENDING CALAMITY...

RELEASE THEIR BONDS! I FEARED ONE DAY OUR UNSTABLE METALS MIGHT CREATE SUCH TERROR!

WE CAN ELIMINATE THE THREAT, SIR...

...BY SKILLFUL DETONATION WE CAN ATOMIZE THE MOUNTAINS WITHOUT DISTURBING YOUR WORLD BELOW!

NO! IT CANNOT BE DONE...

...YOU SEE, THE CHEMISTRY OF THE MOUNTAINS IS WHAT *POWERS* INICRUST! WE *SURVIVE* BY THE MOUNTAINS' FORCE!

THROW FEED SWITCHES!

IT HAS BEEN SO FOR A MILLION MILLION GALAXY YEARS! IT IS OUR LIGHT, HEAT, OXYGEN ....THE POWER TO RUN OUR MACHINES!

CRACKLE! CRACKLE!

...THERE MAY BE ONE... VERY SLIM CHANCE!

SIR, WE WILL RETURN!

EITHER WAY, THE INICRUSTS ARE DOOMED, MR. SPOCK... OUR MISSION HAS... FAILED!

08.4 STAR TIME! LESS THAN 26 HOURS BEFORE COLLISION! NOT A CHANCE TO PREVENT IT!

WAIT! PREPARE TO THROW THE TRANSPORTER SWITCH, CAPTAIN...

AND AS THE CREW BEGINS TO DEMATERIALIZE...

HAVE COURAGE THAT WE CAN SOLVE THE PROBLEM... IN TIME!

AND MOMENTS LATER, AS THEIR BODIES TAKE FORM IN THE TRANSPORTER ROOM OF THE ENTERPRISE...

ONE MOMENT MORE, CAPTAIN!

IN THE NAME OF BLUE THUNDER, SPOCK! --WHAT *IS* THIS SLIM CHANCE?

AS THE FIRST OFFICER HURRIES TO A DEEP GALAXY PROBE SCOPESCREEN...

THANKFUL SATELLITES! IT'S STILL *THERE!*

SPOCK! IS THAT THE LUMINOUS SPACE PARTICLE FROM THE STAR DOONA?

IT *IS*, CAPTAIN! A TRUE WONDER OF THE UNIVERSE...

"WHEN DOONA BECAME A SUPERNOVA AND EXPLODED, ONLY THAT ONE TEN-THOUSAND-TON SECTION FAILED TO DISINTEGRATE...

"FOR CENTURIES, VULCAN SCIENTISTS OF MY PLANET STUDIED THE PHENOMENON...

TEN TIMES THE HARDNESS OF SPACE DIAMONDS...

YES, AND RADIATING A *REPELLING* FORCE OF THE TENTH MAGNITUDE!

HMMM! AND YOU THINK THE REPULSION FORCE **STRONG** ENOUGH TO KEEP F.P.-1 AND F.P.-2 **APART?**

VULCAN EXPERIMENTS INDICATED SO...

...THE DOONA SPACE PARTICLE WAS FOUND TO REACT STRONGLY ON THE KIND OF CHEMICAL CONTENT BOTH PLANETS HAVE! THAT **SLIM** CHANCE....

IF OF COURSE, WE CAN TOW IT BACK HERE IN TIME!

YOUR DECISION, CAPTAIN?

ALL ROCKETS ON FULL! STAR COURSE DEEP GALAXY PENETRATION!

MR. SPOCK, GIVE THEM THE EXACT HEADING! I'LL BE IN THE LAB RIGGING UP AN ELECTRONIC TOW ROPE!

SPOCK DIDN'T SAY IT, BUT HE KNOWS, ALSO---

THAT AREA OF SPACE IS PLAGUED WITH METEOR SWARMS... WE'RE RISKING THE ENTERPRISE AND HER CREW TO SAVE TWO PLANETS!

As after-burners are triggered, the Enterprise pushes close to the speed of light while she hurtles through space on her deadly mission...

Inside the largest, most complex spacecraft in the universe, hundreds of highly trained minds concentrate upon the one problem at hand... *OPERATION SPACE-TOW*...

NCC-1701

NO, NO! THE MAGNETIC TOW LINES MUST HAVE *TWICE* THAT POWER!

WE ARE OFF TIME SCHEDULE SIX MINUTES! JETTISON THE TEN TONS OF ORE SAMPLINGS WE TOOK ON AT GALAXY T-Y!

701

ORE JETTISONED, MR. SPOCK!

EXACTLY EIGHT GALAXY HOURS LATER, ALL IS READY...

CONTACT! WE'VE GOT EXACTLY *FORTY MINUTES* TO LASSO THAT BABY AND START ROCKETING BACK...THOSE PLANETS *COLLIDE* IN THIRTEEN HOURS!

AND WE'LL *NEED* THAT EXTRA RETURN TIME TOWING THAT GLITTERING JOB BEHIND US!

LOAD THE MAGNETIC CARTRIDGE, SCOTTY!

ON TARGET! TURN SHIP INTO A SLOW ORBIT ABOUT OBJECTIVE!

ROUND AND ROUND THE BIZARRE SPACE PARTICLE THE ENTERPRISE SLOWLY ORBITS, WEAVING BANDS OF MAGNETIC POWER...

SWOOOSH BZZZZZZ!

FINALLY....

MAGNETIC MESH NET COMPLETE! CUT CANNON FIRE...SECURE POWER TO ANCHOR-MAGNET!

AYE, AYE, CAPTAIN!

SO FAR, A-OKAY! NOW, WE'VE GOT TO EASE THE ENTERPRISE INTO SPACE-SPEED SLOWLY... A SUDDEN JAR COULD SNAP THE MAGNETIC BONDS!

ROGER, CAPTAIN! WILL DO!

FASTER...FASTER, THE ENTERPRISE MOVES WITH THE LIFE-SAVING PARTICLE IN TOW...

ALL READINGS FINE!

WE'RE DOING GREAT! INCREASE SPEED!

SLOWLY, THE FANTASTIC SHIP INCREASES SPEED ..80,000 MILES A SECOND...100,000 MILES A SECOND...110,000...

THAT'S IT! WITH TEN THOUSAND TONS IN TOW THAT'S OUR TOP SAFETY SPEED! HOLD IT RIGHT THERE!

YES SIR, CAPTAIN KIRK!

BUT THEN, THE FEARED MENACE OF THE SPACE PARTICLE ZONE APPEARS...

METEOR STORM OFF THE STARBOARD BOW!

LIKE HAILSTONES FROM A SPACE HADES, THE RAIN OF STONE AND METAL STRIKES...

WE'RE ENGULFED -- CAUGHT IN THE MIDDLE OF THE STORM!

HURRY WITH THAT COUNTER-PRESSURE WHEEL! LOCK OFF THIS PASSAGE...

...CONTROL! GIVE US TOP SPEED! WE'VE GOT TO GAMBLE OUR WAY THROUGH THIS!

FOR THREE TERROR-STRICKEN MINUTES THE ENTERPRISE, BATTERED AND PUNCTURED, CAREENS THROUGH THE METEOR STORM, UNTIL...

WE ARE THROUGH, CAPTAIN... AND THE MAGNETIC BONDS REPULSED THE METEOR FROM THE PARTICLE.... IT IS SAFE!

WHEW-W-W-W! REDUCE SPEED BEFORE WE RIP THE SHIP APART... AND SOMEBODY BREAK OUT A BARREL OF BLACK COFFEE!

THIRTEEN HOURS LATER, TARGET AND ASSIGNMENT: *PREVENT PLANETARY COLLISION!*..

THERE THEY ARE, CAPTAIN, PLANETS F.P.-1 AND F.P.-2-- *STILL* ON COLLISION COURSE!

WHAT IS THEIR SPEED? HOW MUCH TIME DO WE HAVE?

PRESENT SPEED OF PLANETS 25,000 M.P.H. EARTH MILES... INCREASING... I CALCULATE WE HAVE FOUR GALAXY MINUTES!

NO GOOD! WITH OUR TOW TONNAGE WE'RE TOO SLOW... CONTROL! *FIRE AFTER-BURNERS AGAIN!* THIS IS ALL OUT!

THE SHOWDOWN! WE'LL EITHER GET THERE IN TIME... OR WE'LL BE PULVERIZED BY THE MOST CATACLYSMIC EXPLOSION IN SPACE HISTORY!

WITH EXTRA SPEED FROM THE AFTER-BURNERS, THE SHIP CAREENS INTO SPACE BETWEEN THE TWO PLANETS...BUT THERE IS STILL ONE VITAL QUESTION...

WE MADE IT! BUT HOW, MR. SPOCK, WILL THE REPELLING FORCE *WORK?*

ABRUPTLY, THE SPACE PARTICLE IS CUT LOOSE...ITS REPULSION FORCES RADIATE OUT INTO SPACE...

PRAY, CAPTAIN KIRK... *PRAY!*

FOR A MOMENT, THE ON-RUSHING PLANETS ARE SLOWED, THEY SHUDDER SLIGHTLY IN THEIR DEATH PLUNGE AS THE REPELLING FORCE HITS THEM...

THEN, MAJESTICALLY, THEY BRAKE TO A HALT AND HOVER IN THE SKIES OF SPACE...

IT *WORKED*, MR. SPOCK! THE RAYS ARE SEPARATING THEM! HOW BAD WAS THE SHOCK TO THEM?

PROBABLY QUITE NOTICEABLE, CAPTAIN... LIKE A MODERATE EARTHQUAKE!

BUT, REMEMBER, THERE ARE NO SURFACE BUILDINGS TO TUMBLE ON EITHER PLANET! I AM QUITE CERTAIN ...THEY SURVIVED!

AND SO DID WE! THAT REPELLENT POWER SHOULD HOLD FOR CENTURIES... AND BY THAT TIME PERHAPS THE STAR SHIP ENTERPRISE WILL KNOW HOW TO *REALLY* SOLVE THIS PROBLEM!

PRECISELY MY THINKING, CAPTAIN!

A PAGE FROM SCOTTY'S DIARY

STAR TREK
CHAPTER I
THE VOODOO PLANET
IN ALL THE EXPLORATIONS OF SPACE, THE STAR-SHIP ENTERPRISE HAD NEVER ENCOUNTERED SUCH AN INCREDIBLE SIGHT! IT STAGGERED THE MINDS OF THE MOST SEASONED VOYAGERS... FOR THEY HAD ROCKETED INTO THE MOST TERRIFYING WORLD OF THE UNIVERSE -- ON... THE VOODOO PLANET!
THE EIFFEL TOWER... IT'S TOPPLING! LET'S GET OUT OF HERE, SPOCK--FAST!
I AM HIGHLY IN AGREEMENT, CAPTAIN KIRK...
...AS YOU EARTHLINGS SAY... LET'S MOVE IT!
10210-003
STAR TREK #7-6912

SUDDENLY, ANOTHER PHOTOGRAPH IS BEAMED ONTO THE ENTERPRISE'S SCREEN...

THE STRUCTURE SUDDENLY BUCKLED IN TWO... KILLING HUNDREDS! THE MYSTERIOUS CATASTROPHE OCCURRED AT EXACTLY 12:40 P.M....

12:40 PM EARTH TIME! THAT WAS PRECISELY THE OUTER-GALAXY TIME HERE THAT THE PAPER-MÂCHÉ TOWER TOPPLED ON US!

THEN...THERE'S A *LINK* BETWEEN THE TWO CALAMITIES! IT BEING MERE COINCIDENCE BORDERS ON THE... IMPOSSIBLE!

COULD IT BE SOME SORT OF WEIRD, DEEP SPACE *VOODOO*, I WONDER?

VOODOO? OH YES, THOSE MYSTERIOUS RITES PRACTICED BY CULTS IN WHICH THEY STICK A PIN INTO A DOLL REPRESENTING AN ENEMY... AND HE SUPPOSEDLY DIES!

YES, MR. SPOCK, AND AS A *LASER-BEAM* "PIN" STUCK THE FAKE EIFFEL TOWER THE *REAL* ONE "DIED" ON EARTH!

WHY, THE ENTIRE EARTH COULD BE VOODOOED TO DOOM THAT WAY! WE'VE GOT TO FIND THE SOURCE OF THAT LASER BEAM FAST, MEN!

FLYING BODIES CUT THE AIR SECONDS LATER--AND...

TOO BAD WE COULDN'T USE OUR PHASERS ON THESE CREEPS--BUT THE SOUND WOULD HAVE ATTRACTED THEIR PALS...

SAME DIFFERENCE ...THIS WILL PUT THE GUARDS OUT OF ACTION FOR SOME TIME! NOW LET'S HIT THAT BUILDING ENTRANCE

THE THREE DASH UP A SPIRAL STAIRCASE AND PAUSE...

WHRREEEEE! ZIP! ZIP! ZIP!

ELECTRONIC SOUNDS! I BELIEVE WE HAVE REACHED OUR DESTINATION, CAPTAIN!

BUT THE ROOM MIGHT BE JAMMED WITH...VOODOOITES!

AND AS THE TRIO CREEP UP TO THE DOOR...

SET TIMER! IN MERE SECONDS THE EGYPTIAN SPHINX OF EARTH WILL CRUMBLE BEFORE MY POWER!

PAYDIRT! THEIR CONTROL ROOM-- AND THEY'RE ABOUT TO VOODOO EARTH AGAIN.. THE SPHINX!

IT'S ENTRANCE TIME! DR. McCOY-- YOU'D BETTER BACK US UP OUTSIDE THE DOORWAY HERE WITH PHASER READY! MR. SPOCK AND I WILL GO AHEAD!

ROGER!

THEN...

WE'VE ONLY SECONDS TO SAVE THE SPHINX, MR. SPOCK! LET'S HIT IT!

CONTINUED...

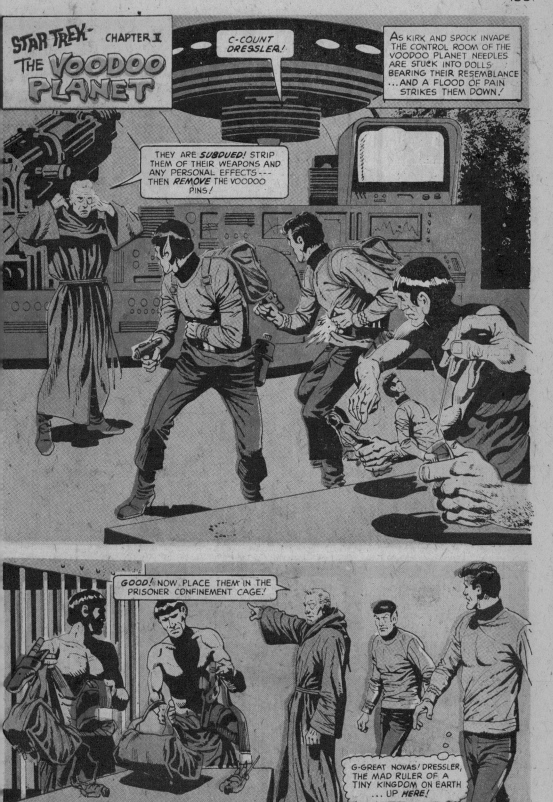

SO *THIS* IS WHERE YOU VANISHED TO WHEN HALF THE WORLD WAS HUNTING YOU DOWN, DRESSLER!

PRECISELY! IT SUITED MY PURPOSES TO FLEE EARTH AT THE TIME!

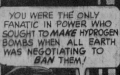

WELL, AT LEAST YOUR INSANE PLAN OF DOMINATING THE WORLD FROM YOUR LITTLE KINGDOM WAS SMASHED!

YOU WERE THE ONLY FANATIC IN POWER WHO SOUGHT TO *MAKE* HYDROGEN BOMBS WHEN ALL EARTH WAS NEGOTIATING TO *BAN* THEM!

HOW *DID* YOU MANAGE IT, DRESSLER? THE LAST I HEARD, THOUSANDS OF TROOPS WERE CLOSING IN ON YOUR KINGDOM!

I WAS QUITE PREPARED, CAPTAIN KIRK!

"WHEN I REALIZED THE ODDS WERE HOPELESS, I MERELY TRIGGERED MY EMERGENCY PLAN-- ROCKET ESCAPE INTO DEEP SPACE..."

"I SOUGHT REFUGE ON ONE OF THE PLANETS HOSTILE TO EARTH'S WAYS! IT WAS MERELY GOOD FORTUNE I CAME UPON THE VOODOO PLANET HERE..."

FRIENDLY SPACE CRUISER REQUESTS LANDING PERMISSION!

IT WAS ONLY A MATTER OF TIME BEFORE I MASTERED THE MINDS OF THESE DOLTS, STOLE THEIR OCCULT SECRETS AND BECAME THEIR LEADER!

BUT *OBSERVE*...YOU ARE JUST IN TIME FOR A *DEMONSTRATION!*

THEN...

WHA...? HE SEEMS TO BE THROWING HIMSELF INTO A *TRANCE* OF SOME KIND!

UNDOUBTEDLY A RITUAL NECESSARY TO PERFORM THE *VOODOO ACT,* CAPTAIN!

ABRUPTLY, A PICTURE FLASHES ON THE SCREEN...

YAA... EEEOOO ...KYA... KYA...

A TV PICTURE OF THE *LEANING TOWER OF PISA!*

OBSERVING HOW THIS CRIMINAL INDUCES VOODOOISM CAN BE TO *OUR* ADVANTAGE!

AND NOW HE'S DRINKING A *GREEN LIQUID!*

HMM...THE LIQUID OBVIOUSLY ACTIVATES HIS VOODOO POWERS IN SOME WAY!

LET'S GET INTO SICK BAY! I'LL INJECT YOU WITH A *PAIN KILLER!* IT SHOULD EASE YOUR SUFFERING...

OH... OH...

AGONIZING MINUTES LATER AFTER THE INJECTIONS.

WELL... ANY RELIEF?

TOLERABLE... AT LEAST I CAN FUNCTION...

THAT CRACKPOT'S REALLY GOT US AT HIS MERCY.

LET'S GET TO THAT OCCULT BOOK OF YOURS, SPOCK-- AND HOPE IT CONTAINS SOMETHING TO STOP HIM!

VERY WELL, CAPTAIN...

THE "WOUNDED" KIRK AND SPOCK ANXIOUSLY SCAN THE PAGES OF THE BOOK FOR HOURS--UNTIL...

HERE IT IS, CAPTAIN... THE VULCAN CLAN WAS KNOWN AS *PAIN CASTERS!*

GO ON, SPOCK-- KEEP READING...

HMM-M... MOST AMAZING -- THE RITUAL PRACTICED BY THE PAIN CASTERS TO INFLICT PHYSICAL HARM IS ALMOST *IDENTICAL* TO THE VOODOO RITES...

A TRANCE-LIKE STATE IS INDUCED BY A MYSTIC CHANT ...A POTION SWALLOWED AND THE POWER OF PAIN CASTING IS INDUCED...

SPOCK! THIS MAY BE OUR SOLUTION...

IF WE COULD *DUPLICATE* THE PAIN CASTERS' POWERS WE COULD TACKLE DRESSLER WITH HIS OWN WEAPON -- VOODOOISM!

DOES IT MENTION THE INGREDIENTS OF THE POTION?

YES, BUT THE HERBS AND CHEMICALS REQUIRED CAN BE FOUND ONLY ON VULCAN...

HOWEVER, I MAY BE ABLE TO PRODUCE *SYNTHETIC* INGREDIENTS!

THEN LET'S GET TO THE LAB AND GO TO WORK!

As THE PAIN CONTINUES TO WRACK THEIR LIMBS, KIRK AND SPOCK FRANTICALLY WORK -- UNTIL FINALLY...

THIS SHOULD DO IT... BUT I CAN PROMISE NOTHING, CAPTAIN!

PUT IT TO THE TEST, SPOCK...

A MOMENT LATER, A KNEELING DR. SPOCK UTTERS STRANGE WORDS...

KA-LOOO... ZHAAAAAA... BROOOO...

IT'S GOT TO WORK, McCOY-- IT'S THE ONLY WAY WE HAVE FOR DEALING WITH THAT MADMAN...

HE'S DRINKING THE POTION! WE'LL SOON KNOW THE ANSWER!

I'VE GOT MY FINGERS CROSSED...

SUDDENLY, THE TENSENESS IS BROKEN AS...

CAPTAIN! THE PAIN IN MY LEG... *IT'S GONE!* THIS MEANS I *POSSESS* THE POWERS OF THE PAIN CASTERS...

HURRY... PERFORM THE RITUAL AS I DID AND RID YOURSELF OF YOUR PAIN!

AND AFTER THE CAPTAIN PERFORMS THE RITUAL...

NO MORE PAIN... WHAT A RELIEF! AND NOW INTO ACTION...

WE'VE GOT TO RETURN TO THE PLANET... DESTROY THAT LASER BEAM AND DEAL WITH DRESSLER! ONLY THIS TIME WE CAN MATCH HIS VOODOO WEAPON WITH *PAIN CASTING!*

I HAVE AN IDEA HOW THAT CAN BE ACCOMPLISHED, CAPTAIN--BUT I WILL REQUIRE A FEW MINUTES.

JOIN ME IN THE TRANSPORTER CHAMBER ...

SHORTLY...

REMEMBER, WE WANT TO MATERIALIZE RIGHT *IN* DRESSLER'S LAB!

YES SIR!

AND AS THE MATERIALIZING FORMS OF THE CAPTAIN AND SPOCK APPEAR IN DRESSLER'S LABORATORY...

YOU TWO... BACK AGAIN, EH? I DON'T KNOW WHY YOU'RE NOT IN UTTER PAIN...

BUT THIS TIME I SHALL KILL YOU WITH MY VOODOO POWERS!

DON'T COUNT ON IT, DRESSLER!

TERROR CROSSES THE FACE OF THE CRIMINAL AN INSTANT LATER AS...

I-I PIERCED THE HEAD OF YOUR DOLL WITH MY PIN AND YOU STILL *LIVE*, KIRK! I'M... *POWERLESS!*

YOUR CAUSE IS HOPELESS, DRESSLER--YOUR DAYS OF BLACKMAILING EARTH ARE OVER...

FOR YOU SEE, *WE* NOW POSSESS THE SAME OCCULT POWERS YOU HAVE--AND WE'RE GOING TO GIVE YOU A SAMPLE...

PRICK A SHOULDER OF THE DRESSLER DOLL YOU MADE AND LET HIM KNOW HOW IT FEELS, SPOCK...

A PLEASURE, CAPTAIN...

SPOCK! IT HAD *NO* AFFECT ON HIM! I DON'T UNDERSTAND...

WE WEREN'T THINKING, CAPTAIN! DRESSLER IS IMMUNE TO OUR PAIN POWERS BECAUSE THE VOODOO POTION HE TOOK IS STILL IN HIS SYSTEM...

JUST AS *WE* NEUTRALIZED HIS VOODOO POWERS AFTER WE SWALLOWED OUR POTION!

WE MUST OVERTAKE DRESSLER, CAPTAIN! IF WE CAN GET CLOSE ENOUGH TO HIM *WE* CAN TRANSPORT HIM UP TO THE ENTERPRISE AS OUR PRISONER...

BUT FIRST WE'VE GOT TO KNOCK THAT LASER BEAM OUT!

BOOOM

OUTSIDE, AS KIRK AND SPOCK ATTEMPT TO RUN DOWN THE CRIMINAL...

GUARDS! GUARDS! SEIZE THESE ENEMIES OF OURS-- CUT THEM DOWN!

WE'RE NOT *CLOSE* ENOUGH TO TRANSPORT DRESSLER TO THE SHIP...AND THOSE GUARDS WILL BE ON US IN SECONDS...

SUDDENLY THE UNEXPECTED HAPPENS...

LOOK! DRESSLER'S STOPPED IN HIS TRACKS...AND HE'S CLUTCHING HIS SHOULDER AS IF IN PAIN!

OUR PAIN CASTING IS AFFECTING HIM! NOW I UNDERSTAND...

THE POTION THAT PROTECTED HIM FROM OUR POWERS HAS WORN OFF...HE'S NO LONGER IMMUNE...

AND NOW HE'S FEELING THE EFFECT OF THE PIN JAB WE GAVE HIS DOLL!

WELL, LET'S GET CLOSE ENOUGH TO TRANSPORT HIM TO THE SHIP BEFORE ONE OF THE VOODOO RAY BLASTS CALL US BY NAME!

A MOMENT LATER, KIRK RADIOS FOR THE TRANSPORTER BEAM, AND...

WHEW! THAT WAS CLOSE-- WE'RE GETTING OUT OF HERE JUST IN THE NICK OF TIME!

AND ABOARD THE STAR SPACESHIP ENTERPRISE...

I SUPPOSE A QUICK TRIAL AND EXECUTION WILL BE MY FATE...

WE HAVE BETTER PLANS FOR YOU, COUNT DRESSLER-- A FATE BEFITTING YOUR EVIL!

WE HAVE A PLANET IN MIND FOR YOU-- ONE ON WHICH YOU CAN SUSTAIN YOURSELF BUT WHERE THERE IS NO LIVING BEING YOU CAN HARM!

A-A PLANETARY PRISON... I'LL GO MAD!

YOU MIGHT CALL IT SOLITARY CONFINEMENT, DRESSLER!

Profile of an Artist

Alberto Giolitti

As comic buffs know, Alberto Giolitti was not the original STAR TREK artist. That distinction belongs to Nevio Zaccara. Other commitments forced Nevio to give it up after the second issue and Alberto took over.

Alberto lives and works in Rome, his native city. However, right after the war, he went on an artist's odyssey that kept him away from his home town for a dozen years. During that time, he settled down in various places, among them, Buenos Aires, New York, Lake George, Florida. When he first came to New York, he spoke little English. Most of the time he stayed in his apartment, alone, and worked, leaving the radio on all the time so he could keep listening to the local language. Eventually he couldn't stand it. He had to get out and hear and speak some Italian. So he took the subway down to Little Italy in Greenwich Village. He couldn't understand a word they were saying. Today he speaks a fluent English with the warm Latin accent and inflections reminiscent of Marcello Mastroianni. And back in Rome he has no trouble understanding their Italian.

What is the unmistakable stamp that characterizes his work? First, he is a superlative draftsman, with a bold, sure ink line. Second, his placement of solid blocks in a panel and on a page are carefully planned to hold the drawing together. Moreover, he is a tireless researcher. His studio has shelves and file cabinets filled with drawings and photos which he has used, will use or might someday use. He has a prop room with guns, spears, shields, hats, saddles and other articles he'll be copying. No wonder every scene has the look of authenticity.

But he doesn't slavishly depend on his reference material. Rather he adapts his references to heighten the dramatic or artistic or narrative value of his drawing. It is always a distinct pleasure for the reader when Alberto has decided that the story is best told with a panel rich in detail where every corner has some impeccably rendered object. He approaches systematically the drawing of a story. After he reads it, he will go over it in his mind to visualize what positions he will need for his figures. Then he takes out his camera and makes photographs of every figure he will need. His models: friends, fellow artists, acquaintances, but most of all, himself. Sometimes he shoots as many as a hundred pictures for a single comic book. That's why every one of his figures is not only perfectly drawn—it also has character, attitude, so natural that it looks as if it is going to walk right off the page.

Still, one day several years ago, an editor for Gold Key Comics was looking over some Giolitti artwork freshly arrived from Rome. It was, as usual, superb. But then, on page six, he saw something that made his mouth hang open in horrified disbelief. His agonized scream brought people from everywhere on the 15th floor rushing to his office to help. Speechless, all he could do was point. There it was— a beautifully drawn figure, but out of the left sleeve came a RIGHT hand. No one, least of all Alberto himself, was ever able to explain how such an error was made.

STAR TREK — THE YOUTH TRAP

PART I

THE CREW OF THE ENTERPRISE FIND THEMSELVES GUINEA PIGS FOR A CRAZED ALIEN WHO POSSESSES A FANTASTIC MACHINE! AND IT APPEARS THAT NO POWER IN THE UNIVERSE CAN PREVENT THE BIZARRE TRANSFORMATION OF CAPTAIN KIRK'S MEN AS ONE BY ONE, THEY BEGIN AN INCREDIBLE RETURN TO INFANCY!

SUFFERING SUN SPOTS — OUR TWO ENGINEERS...THEY'VE BEEN REDUCED TO FIVE-YEAR-OLDS!

YES, CAPTAIN! AND THAT TEEN-AGER — IT IS DR. McCOY AS A YOUTH!

Captain's Log, Stardate 31:09.5 . . . . DATA REF. . . . 8.00-8.26

A MICRO-SECOND LATER, SPACE ORE EXPERTS BURNS AND LANE MATERIALIZE ON THE UNCHARTED PLANET...

THERE'S A GOOD ROCK OUTCROPPING TO START OUR ORE SAMPLING WITH!

ROGER!

FOR AN HOUR THE EXPERTS CHIP AWAY AT DIFFERENT SECTIONS OF THE SPACE ROCK, THEN...

BURNS TO SHIP! FIRST SAMPLES N.G. -- TESTING REMAINING ROCKS!

CLICK! CLICK!

HOT NOVAS! WE'VE GOT IT--THESE CHUNKS ARE CHOCK FULL OF ZUTOTANIUM, CAPTAIN KIRK!

BUT SUDDENLY AS KIRK REPLIES FROM THE ENTERPRISE...

GOOD! PREPARE SAMPLES FOR TRANSPORTATION BACK AND KEEP DIGGING...

BURNS...LANE! WHAT WAS THAT SOUND? ARE YOU ALL RIGHT?

THEY ARE OUT OF SCANNER VIEW BEHIND THE LEDGE, CAPTAIN!

TENSION RISES IN THE ENTERPRISE AS LONG SECONDS PASS WITHOUT A RESPONSE FROM THE PAIR, AND FINALLY...

ENTERPRISE TO ORE EXPEDITION TEAM! COME IN! COME IN!

LISTEN!

206

YOUR SIDEKICK KOOBA --HE'S TAKING OFF WITH THE MACHINE! WHY DID HE ATTACK YOU UP THERE, ANYWAY?

I CANNOT SAY! BUT HE IS MOVING IN THE DIRECTION OF OUR ENCAMPMENT!

AND IT'S A CINCH HE'S UP TO NO GOOD...

LET'S MOVE--WE'RE ALL AT THAT CHARACTER'S MERCY AS LONG AS HE HAS POSSESSION OF THE AGE-RAY MACHINE!

AS DUSK SETTLES OVER THE PLANET, THE TRIO MAKES ITS WAY TO A ROCK LEDGE WHERE,...

LISTEN WELL...THE SCIENTIST LAIKO IS NO MORE! AND I NOW PLACE MYSELF IN ABSOLUTE COMMAND OF THIS EXPEDITION! YOU WILL DO MY BIDDING OR ELSE!

MOST DISCOURAGING! I FEAR THAT EVIL BEING INTENDS TO USE THE AGE-RAY AS A WEAPON AGAINST HIS OWN PEOPLE!

211

THE BIZARRE SLED BARRELS DOWN THE HILLSIDE AND INTO THE ALIEN GROUP WHERE FISTS FLY...

LOOKS LIKE WE'VE GOT OUR HANDS FULL, SPOCK! WHAT IS OUR CHANCE OF NAILING THAT MACHINE AND ESCAPING?

NIL, CAPTAIN!

SEIZE THEM! THEY ARE HOSTILE... INVADERS FROM ANOTHER GALAXY!

WHY DON'T YOU ALL COME TO YOUR SENSES! YOUR REAL ENEMY IS KOOBA... AND THIS IS YOUR CHANCE TO OVERTHROW HIM!

IT IS NO USE, CAPTAIN KIRK--FOR THEY FEAR YOUR PRESENCE MORE THAN THEY DO THAT CULPRIT!

AND WHEN THE WEIGHT OF SHEER NUMBERS FINALLY TAKES ITS TOLL...

EXCELLENT! BRING THEM BEFORE ME FOR SENTENCING!

WELL, WE LOOKED GOOD WHILE IT LASTED, SPOCK!

AND I FEAR THE WORST IS YET TO COME, CAPTAIN!

STAR TREK—
PART II
THE YOUTH TRAP

FATE HAS PLACED CAPTAIN KIRK, SPOCK AND THE ALIEN LAIKO AT THE MERCY OF KOOBA AND THE FANTASTIC AGE-RAY MACHINE! AND NOW THE PRISONERS HEAR THEIR SENTENCE...

I WILL HAVE THE THREE OF YOU EXECUTED IN DUE TIME! BUT FOR THE MOMENT YOU ARE MORE VALUABLE TO ME ALIVE...

ONE THING PUZZLES ME--WHY WASN'T I AFFECTED BY THAT AGE-RAY BLAST WHEN IT HIT ME?

BUT YOU *WERE,* YOU FOOL! A MATTER OF SEVERAL MONTHS PERHAPS!

IN OTHER WORDS, WITH REPEATED DOSES AT REGULAR INTERVALS, I CAN REMAIN *THIS AGE* WITH MY FULL MENTAL CAPACITY...FOREVER!

YES...BUT OF COURSE I WON'T LET YOU! WHEN IT SUITS MY PURPOSE I'LL TURN YOU TOO INTO AN INFANT!

COME TO YOUR SENSES, KOOBA! WHAT DO YOU HOPE TO GAIN BY HOLDING THAT MACHINE OVER THE HEADS OF OUR COLONY HERE?

KOOBA TRIGGERS THE AGE-RAY MACHINE--AND AS THE TV CIRCUIT CARRIES THE BLAST THROUGH THE SHIP, THE ENTERPRISE LIGHTS UP LIKE A CHRISTMAS TREE...

KA-FUUUM!

THE RESULTS ARE INSTANTLY KNOWN...

THE ACID SCAR I ACQUIRED IN THE PALM OF MY HAND SOME FOUR YEARS AGO --IT HAS VANISHED!

THOSE FAINT LINES UNDER MY EYES... THEY'VE DISAPPEARED!

BOOMIN' BAG-PIPES--SOME OF MY HAIR'S RETURNED TO MY HEAD!

YOUR LITTLE EXPERIMENT WORKED TO A DEGREE, KOOBA --BUT YOU HARDLY TRANSFORMED US INTO HELPLESS BABIES!

YOU ARE A MAN OF SCIENCE, SPOCK.--THINK! OBVIOUSLY THE TV RELAY OF THE BLAST ONLY SLOWED DOWN THE TRANSFORMATION PROCESS...

THE ORIGINAL BLAST DE-AGED YOU ALL SOME FIVE OR SO YEARS! NOW YOU WILL ALL SLOWLY GROW YOUNGER...

IN A MATTER OF HOURS YOU WILL ALL BE BABES ...UNABLE TO COMPREHEND YOUR DIRE SITUATION!

THAT SHINY TIN PLATE... I WONDER?
THEN, AS ANOTHER BLAST SEEKS OUT KIRK...
IT WORKED...THE SHINY PLATE REFLECTED THE RAY BLAST!
YIIIII!
A CLEVER MANEUVER, CAPTAIN! BUT YOU ARE ONLY *DELAYING* YOUR FATE--IT IS IMPOSSIBLE TO REFLECT EVERY RAY I FIRE AT YOU!
HE'S RIGHT... IF I DON'T NAIL HIM NOW I'M FINISHED!
THEN, AS ANOTHER BLAST WITH KIRK'S NAME ON IT STREAKS THROUGH THE AIR...
IF I CAN REFLECT THIS BLAST AT JUST THE RIGHT ANGLE...
ZIIINNG

VERY TRUE, LAIKO! BUT PERHAPS WE CAN LEAD HIM TO *BELIEVE* HE IS TRANSPORTING KOOBA TO THE ENTERPRISE...

I'VE GOT AN IDEA THAT'S WORTH TRYING! LET'S HURRY...

A SHORT TIME LATER, TWO FIGURES MATERIALIZE IN THE TRANSPORTATION CHAMBER OF THE ENTERPRISE...

I SEE YOU HAVE MADE PEACE WITH LAIKO, KOOBA!

YES, WE ARE FRIENDS ONCE AGAIN, GORG...

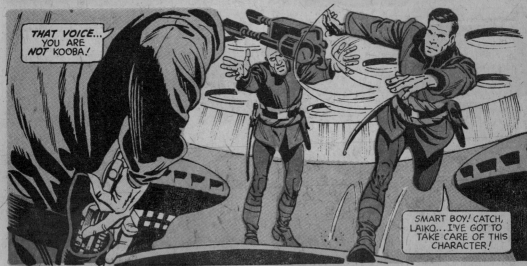

THAT VOICE... YOU ARE *NOT* KOOBA!

SMART BOY! CATCH, LAIKO... I'VE GOT TO TAKE CARE OF THIS CHARACTER!

LAIKO! UNBOLT THE CHAMBER DOOR! I WANT TO MAKE CONTACT WITH MY CREW...

OOF!

WELL, CALL THEM IN! WHAT'S WRONG, LAIKO?

I-I THINK YOU HAD BETTER SEE FOR YOURSELF, CAPTAIN!

224